2.95

WRITERS AND CRITICS

||||||||||||||||||||||||||||||||||

Chief Editors

A. NORMAN JEFFARES
R. L. C. LORIMER

H. G. WELLS

PATRICK PARRINDER

Capricorn Books

G.P. Putnam's Sons, New York

823.912
Wel

1/27/82
Dinosaur Disc .59

First American Edition

COPYRIGHT © 1970, 1977 by Patrick Parrinder
All rights reserved. This book, or parts thereof, may
not be reproduced in any form without permission.
Published simultaneously in Canada by Longman Canada
Limited, Toronto.

SBN: 399-50377-3

Library of Congress Cataloging in Publication Data

Parrinder, Patrick, comp.
  H. G. Wells.

  Bibliography
  Includes index.
  1. Wells, Herbert George, 1866-1946—Criticism and
interpretation. I. Title.
PR5777.P37 1977   823'.9'12   76-52378

PRINTED IN THE UNITED STATES OF AMERICA

39533
SUE BENNETT COLLEGE LIBRARY

ACKNOWLEDGMENTS

Acknowledgments are due to the University of Illinois Library for supplying a copy of the typescript of "Mr Wells Explains Himself".

Thanks are due to A. P. Watt and Son, agents for the Wells Estate, for quotations from the works of H. G. Wells.

I should also like to express my thanks to Raymond Williams for his encouragement and criticism at all stages of my work on Wells, and to Eric Homberger for his painstaking comments on my typescript.

TO MY PARENTS

CONTENTS

ABBREVIATED TITLES BY WHICH SOME OF H. G. WELLS'S WORKS ARE CITED IN THE TEXT

Since there is no generally available standard edition, references to Wells's novels are given by chapter and section only, except in the case of *The Complete Short Stories*.

Atlantic Edn.	=	*The Atlantic Edition of the Works of H. G. Wells*, 28 vols.
A.V.	=	*Ann Veronica.*
C.S.S.	=	*The Complete Short Stories of H. G. Wells.*
E.A.	=	*Experiment in Autobiography.*
F.M.M.	=	*The First Men in the Moon.*
I.M.	=	*The Invisible Man.*
K.	=	*Kipps.*
L.L.	=	*Love and Mr Lewisham.*
Moreau	=	*The Island of Dr Moreau.*
M.U.	=	*A Modern Utopia.*
N.M.	=	*The New Machiavelli.*
P.	=	*The History of Mr Polly.*
T.B.	=	*Tono-Bungay.*
W.A.	=	*The War in the Air.*
W.V.	=	*The Wonderful Visit.*
W.W.	=	*The War of the Worlds.*

I

AN INTELLECTUAL OUTLINE

H. G. Wells (1866–1946) has been described as "the most serious of the popular writers of his time, and the most popular of the serious".[1] One of this century's most prolific and versatile writers, his imaginative hold over his contemporaries was such that George Orwell did not exaggerate unduly when he wrote that:

> Thinking people who were born about the beginning
> of this century are in some sense Wells's own creation.
> How much influence any mere writer has, and
> especially a "popular" writer whose work takes effect
> quickly, is questionable, but I doubt whether anyone who
> was writing books between 1900 and 1920, at any rate
> in the English language, influenced the young so
> much. The minds of all of us, and therefore the physical
> world, would be perceptibly different if Wells had never
> existed.[2]

Yet this was written in 1941, when the young minds, given shape and direction by reading Wells, had passed beyond him, while their ageing teacher had gone on repeating himself with an apparently inexhaustible energy which was less and less associated with creative genius. Orwell added that "just the singleness of mind, the one-sided imagination that made him seem like an inspired prophet in the Edwardian age, make him a shallow, inadequate thinker now". He was concerned with the side of Wells which was most in evidence in 1941; Wells as journalist, popular champion of "science" against "reaction", and prophet of a future world state. Orwell's argument was that Wells's rationalistic influence weakened the defences against Hitler and totalitarianism; he was "too sane to understand the modern world"[3] of militarism and organised evil. It is a criticism which for many seemed to be borne out by the abrupt reversal into despair of Wells's final book, *Mind at the End of its Tether* (1945). Early in the war he had poured contempt on the German army and air force and predicted their imminent collapse; but the atrocities of the concentration camp and the atomic bomb could no longer be blamed on a single lunatic dictator. In a sober and curiously wooden "scientific" prose Wells now wrote that the whole human species, and not just the things he had opposed, was an anachronism; it had failed to adapt to its environment, and its extinction was now at hand. He has not, of course, been proved wrong; but precisely his "singleness of mind" appeared to have led him into such a drastic and disabling loss of faith, and although many of the causes he championed will continue to seem honourable and even inevitable for human progress, since *Mind at the End of its Tether* the influence he once commanded as a thinker has never seemed likely to return.

And yet such reversals of hope and despair, of control and submission, of deification and extinction, had dominated Wells's imagination, and inspired its moments of intense vision, drama and irony, since his earliest days as a writer. As the incessant journalism of his later years recedes from our view, his deeper and more permanent contribution to his age has been found in the novels and scientific romances he wrote before 1910. It is still necessary to salvage them, as several critics have recently done, from the ruins of the public edifice into which Orwell threw his well-aimed hand grenade. Consider his analysis of Wells's value-system:

> On the one side science, order, progress, internationalism, aeroplanes, steel, concrete, hygiene: on the other side war, nationalism, religion, monarchy, peasants, Greek professors, poets, horses. History as he sees it is a series of victories won by the scientific man over the romantic man.[4]

The simple and brutal antithesis does indeed sum up much of the faith which Wells inspired in his roles of educationalist, moralist, and political journalist. But even here, I would suggest, the faith was complicated by a legend, a force of personality which Scott Fitzgerald recorded when he wrote of "the gloriously intoxicated efforts of H. G. Wells to fit the key of romantic symmetry into the elusive lock of truth".[5] It is far from certain that the "scientific man" won in Wells himself. Complete "singleness of mind" would probably be disastrous for a novelist, and the imaginative cast of Wells as a living artist is essentially ambiguous and complex.

Late in 1895, the year of his first literary successes, Wells sketched out a brief autobiography at the request of one of his publishers:

> I was born at a place called Bromley in Kent, a suburb
> of the damnedest, in 1866, educated at a beastly little
> private school there until I was thirteen, apprenticed on
> trial to all sorts of trades, attracted the attention of
> a man called Byatt, Headmaster of Midhurst Grammar
> School, by the energy with which I mopped up Latin—I
> went to him for Latin for a necessary examination
> while apprenticed (on approval, of course!) to a chemist
> there, became a kind of teaching scholar to him, got a
> scholarship at the Royal College of Science, S. Kensington
> (1884), worked there three years, started a students'
> journal, read abundantly in the Dyce and Foster Library,
> failed my last year's examination (geology), wandered
> in the wilderness of private school teaching, had a
> lung haemorrhage, got a London degree B.Sc. (1889) with
> first- and second-class honours, private coaching,
> *Globe* turnovers, article in the *Fortnightly* (1890), edited an
> obscure educational paper, had haemorrhage for the
> second time (1893), chucked coaching and went for
> journalism.[6]

The texture of the experiences hinted at here can be found in novels like *Tono-Bungay* and *Mr Polly* and in Wells's *Experiment in Autobiography* (1934). The *Autobiography* remains the best account of his life as well as the most engaging statement of many of his opinions. But in a sense the novels tell us even more, for Wells has the gift of making his readers see, in his own life, a representative and almost mythical significance. Take the curt reference to Bromley, "a suburb of the damnedest". Wells grew up there in a small china shop, known as Atlas House, with tortuous staircases and a cramped, underground kitchen. His mother had been a lady's maid, and his father was a gardener and professional cricketer who had saved and borrowed enough capital to set up on his own. The shop did not pay, and after a few years the family split up to avoid facing bankruptcy. Wells's fiction reveals this precarious world of retail trade, at the lower edge of the lower middle class, as one of the characteristic sources of English social consciousness. It is a shabby world, clinging to the illusion of gentility, and combining the deference of servant-hood with a jealously-guarded sense of respectability and status; a world where personal identity becomes a bulwark against the threatening, anonymous crowd around and below, and where the nearness of the crowd, and the fear of catching one's own reflexion in it, can lead to a social outlook tinged with hysterical uncharity. George Ponderevo, the hero of *Tono-Bungay*, is not entirely innocent of this:

> My uncle and aunt seemed to me to be leading . . . *dingy*
> lives. They seemed to be adrift in a limitless crowd of
> dingy people, wearing shabby clothes, living uncomfortably
> in shabby second-hand houses, going to and fro on
> pavements that had always a thin veneer of greasy, slippery
> mud, under grey skies that showed no gleam of hope
> of anything for them but dinginess until they died.[7]

The people around one become as dingy as their surroundings. The effects of petty bourgeois frustration are symbolised by Mr Polly's dyspepsia, and his consequent loss of "human kindliness".[8] The typical artists produced by this world are Dickens and Wells, generous rebels whose anger and laughter, and whose love of the colourful and the grotesque, are an extreme reaction against drabness and isolation.

Mr Polly is the archetypal figure of Wells's lower-class world, an apprentice shop-assistant who becomes a small shopkeeper and finally escapes into a more humane and open existence. He is the creation of a man who rose above his own class and apparent destiny. Both Polly and Kipps subdue themselves to the social trap for long periods; Wells was deeply marked by a similar experience in a much shorter time. At fifteen he began working a thirteen-hour day in a drapery store at Southsea, sleeping in a dormitory above the shop and enjoying an hour and a half of free time a day. But after two miserable years he was offered the position of "teaching scholar" at Midhurst Grammar School, and left the drapery without notice. The traces of his subjection and escape are not confined to his social comedies; they can be found in all his early novels. The idea of release from a limiting environment, or "disentanglement" as Robert P. Weeks has called it,[9] constantly recurs. Two images of life are implied by it: the first a life of subjection to the environment, the second of control over it. The one leads to a deterministic view of present society, the other to a utopian vision of human freedom and fulfilment. The process of release or escape which joins the two takes many different forms, from scientific inventions such as the Time Machine and the technology of the Martians, to the instinctive rebellions of Kipps and Polly and the "constructive revolution" envisaged in Wells's political thought. Reviewing Wells's early struggles, including his battle against illness in the 1890s, C. P. Snow wrote that "This wasn't a life many of us would have come through intact".[10] Wells's novels return again and again to the need for transcending the given conditions, and in his propaganda works he seems to be willing his own instinct for survival and growth, and perhaps also his luck, on to the whole human species.

Wells confirmed his escape by becoming a novelist. This is how he put it in an article published in 1911:

The literary life is one of the modern forms of adventure. Success with a book—even such a commercially modest success as mine has been—means in the English-speaking world not merely a moderate financial independence

but the utmost freedom of movement and intercourse.
One is lifted out of one's narrow circumstances into
familiar and unrestrained intercourse with a great variety
of people. One sees the world.[11]

Success for him brought intellectual nourishment as well as
material comforts. This suggests that his way of "seeing the world"
had little in common with that of most modern novelists. We
may compare a statement from his *Autobiography*:

So much of my life has been a prolonged and enlarged
adolescence, an encounter with the world in general,
that the observation of character began to play a leading
part in it only in my later years. It was necessary for me
to reconstruct the frame in which individual lives as a
whole had to be lived, before I could concentrate upon
any of the individual problems of fitting them into
this frame.[12]

It is helpful to contrast this with Joseph Conrad's belief that
whereas the scientist and the thinker are concerned with the
external "aspect of the world", the artist "descends within himself" to win the truth from "that lonely region of stress and
strife".[13] By comparison with James, Conrad, Lawrence, Joyce,
and Virginia Woolf (all of whom were his friends or acquaintances)
Wells was among the scientists and thinkers. He began by writing
scientific romances (this term, implying a scientific subdivision of
the form practised by Hawthorne, Stevenson, Rider Haggard, and
others, has now been superseded by "science fiction", but I have
retained it as the more expressive of the two). They were an
imaginative response to the transformation in our understanding
and control of the external world which is the dominating feature
of modern civilisation. Scientific romance is connected with spec-
ulation and with the generalising and synthesising tendencies of
the mind; beyond its particular excitements and fears it develops
a sense of the universe rather than a sense of the self. Wells's
stories are derived, not by conscious extension from his own
observations and experience, but by selecting a focus within his

"reconstruction" of the whole physical, organic, and human frame. The process of reconstruction was his most important activity during the twelve years which separated his escape from the drapery, and his emergence as a writer and journalist.

Wells began to "see the world" on visits to his mother. She had become housekeeper at Uppark, the Augustan country house on the Sussex downs which is portrayed as Bladesover in *Tono-Bungay*. Bladesover is described as a "complete authentic microcosm"[14] of traditional England; Wells's view from "below stairs" gave him both a key for interpreting the social structure of his time, and an insight into the faded country house culture which, he later wrote, had produced "the Royal Society, the *Century of Inventions*, the first museums and laboratories and picture galleries, gentle manners, good writing, and nearly all that is worth while in our civilisation today".[15] The greatest personal disappointment of his life was his exclusion from the Royal Society. From the eighteenth-century civilisation revealed at Uppark Wells took ideals of spaciousness and intellectual freedom; the classless Utopia of his late romance *Men like Gods* (1923) is a parkland inhabited by the genteel scientists of a new Age of Reason.

The library at Uppark had been built by a freethinker, and here Wells quietly made his way through neglected editions of Swift, Voltaire, Dr Johnson, Tom Paine, and Gibbon. He found a telescope, volumes of Michelangelo and Raphael engravings, and Plato's *Republic*, which, he says, prompted "the amazing and heartening suggestion that the whole fabric of law, custom and worship, which seemed so invincibly established, might be cast into the melting pot and made anew".[16] He also read Henry George's *Progress and Poverty*, an economic treatise which had a great influence on the socialists of the 1880s. Here he found the ideas that industrialism had reduced men to a state of brutal subjection, and that the development of civilisation was fast leading to a crisis which could only be overcome by social reorganisation. George's attack on capitalist injustice may have led to Wells's conversion to socialism, and to the symbolic act of wearing a blood-red tie: but perhaps even more important were the American thinker's speculations about "The Law of Human Progress"

and the rise and fall of civilisations. In 1884 Wells went to South
Kensington to be trained as a science teacher. In his first year he
took anatomy and zoology under T. H. Huxley, the great biologist, essayist, and champion of Darwin's evolutionary theory.
"Social Darwinism", a series of muddled attempts to apply evolutionary thinking in the social and political sphere, was becoming
fashionable. It would have been surprising if Wells, now living
on a meagre grant of a guinea a week, did not apply the "survival
of the fittest" to his own case; and after following the evolution
of living organisms stage by stage in his microscopy and dissec-
tions, he was able to boast that he "had man definitely placed in
the great scheme of space and time".[17] He gained a first-class mark
at the end of the first year, but in the next two years, doing physics
and geology, his attention wandered. The books he read—Goethe,
Carlyle, Shelley, Blake, Shakespeare, Confucius—suggest a
reaction against scientific education; he argued vigorously in
college debates, fell in love with his cousin, and failed his final
examination in 1887. Wells's interest in science was primarily a
speculative one. Once he had grasped the general scheme of the
universe and man's place in it, he was prepared to leave the
laborious accumulation of physical details to others. Evolutionary
theory, however, became the fundamental constituent of his
intellectual understanding, and he became deeply involved in the
intellectual revaluation brought about by the new perspectives of
biology. All sorts of apologists were drawing upon Darwin's
theories of natural selection and of human origins to vindicate
physical, economic or military "competition" between individuals, classes, nations, and racial groups. The classic and authoritative response to this welter of theory was Huxley's Romanes
Lecture *Evolution and Ethics* (1893). Wells's own contribution came
in two articles in the *Fortnightly Review* during 1896–7, entitled
"Human Evolution, An Artificial Process" and "Morals and
Civilisation". These stand as a prologue to his social thought, and,
as W. Warren Wagar has noted in his excellent study of Wells
as a thinker,[18] they are permeated by the influence of Huxley.

Both Huxley and Wells found themselves obliged to combat
the feeling that the drama of natural evolution provided no role

for constructive human action to play. The religious opponents of
Darwinism felt that kinship with the apes meant a degradation of
human stature and achievement, while the apologists tended to
explain the progress of civilisation by the laws of the economic or
military jungle. In *Evolution and Ethics* Huxley argued that conflicts in civilised human communities are generally different from
the conflicts of organisms in the natural state. Men struggle, not
for existence, but for the "means of enjoyment".[19] Social progress
takes place in opposition to the cosmic evolutionary process, and it
is measured in ethical and not biological terms. Wells begins
"Human Evolution" with a more specific attack on the vulgar
errors of Social Darwinism; the assumption that natural selection
could have had measurable effects on humanity in the short period
since the Stone Age, for example, is biologically unsound. Instead,
the development of civilisation is an "artificial process" completely
divorced from genetics:

> in civilised man we have (1) an inherited factor, the
> natural man, who is the product of natural selection, the
> culminating ape, and a type of animal more obstinately
> unchangeable than any other living creature; and (2)
> an acquired factor, the highly plastic creature of tradition,
> suggestion and reasoned thought.[20]

The acquired or artificial factor proceeded originally from the
invention of speech, and it is "the one reality of civilisation". In
"Morals and Civilisation", Wells characteristically evokes a vision
of its sudden disappearance. Cities, railways, and factories stand
deserted, and men are plunged back into predatory conflict and
the primal emotions of comradeship, sexuality, anger, and fear.
(Similar prophecies of social collapse can be found in *The War
of the Worlds*, "A Story of the Days to Come" and *The War in
the Air*.) The two essays are not pessimistic in tone, however.
Civilisation is precarious, but it is also, unlike natural evolution,
amenable to the control of a collective will. The quality of a whole
society is an aggregate of the qualities of the artificial factors in
individuals, and these factors are the products of social education.
By refusing to accept the deterministic view of evolution, Wells

in effect reaffirms the traditional view that social advancement is
the responsibility of the educator and the politician—a necessary
prelude to a lifetime of campaigning activity. At the same time,
he continued to think of humanity in biological terms. Huxley
had recognised that what he called the "ethical process" came
within the natural orbit, and he illustrated his conception by the
rather imperfect image of the governor which is part of the steam-
engine. A governor has a regulating action, ensuring even motion,
as (in another of Huxley's metaphors) a gardener weeds a flower-
bed. But Wells's "artificial process" is itself evolutionary and
subject to flux. One of his innovations was the rejection of the
static, millennial idea of utopia:

> The Utopia of a modern dreamer must needs differ
> in one fundamental aspect from the Nowheres and
> Utopias men planned before Darwin quickened the thought
> of the world. Those were all perfect and static States,
> a balance of happiness won for ever against the forces of
> unrest and disorder that inhere in things. . . . Change and
> development were dammed back by invincible dams
> for ever. But the Modern Utopia must be not static but
> kinetic, must shape not as a permanent state but as a
> hopeful stage, leading to a long ascent of stages.[21]

Wells wrote several versions of Utopia, and some people have
believed that this was because he could never convince himself of
any one of them. But Mark R. Hillegas[22] is surely right in arguing
that books like *The World Set Free*, *A Modern Utopia*, and *Men
Like Gods* describe widely separate stages of the historical ascent.
The summit is never seen. An unrecognisable physical evolution,
brought about by eugenics rather than natural selection, is often
implied. The Martians in *The War of the Worlds*, for example, are
not the bug-eyed stereotypes of the horror film but a fantasy
based on the atrophy of all human organs except the brain and
hands; they were developed from an earlier sketch entitled "The
Man of the Year Million". In *The Discovery of the Future* Wells
coined a vague, spectacular phrase for man's cosmic potential
which he often repeated:

a day will come ... when beings, ... who are now latent
in our thoughts and hidden in our loins, shall stand
upon this earth as one stands upon a footstool, and shall
laugh and reach out their hands amid the stars.[23]

Wells did sometimes suggest space-travel as the ultimate human
achievement, but this and other visions are really only carrots to
persuade humanity to get on with organising and planning the
next stage, and he was equally alive to the intimations of catastrophe, even if he sometimes preferred to suppress them. His later
works propound a sort of evolutionary mysticism to take the
place of theocratic religion. On the whole this is no more than an
intellectual curiosity, but it has the importance of underwriting
his immediate political and social aims with consistent moral
attitudes and beliefs about individuality which play an important
part in his novels.

As I have indicated, one of the effects of Darwin's thought was
to give a wholly new breadth of implication to the old question
of the "higher" and "lower" elements in human nature. In
"Morals and Civilisation" Wells imagined humanity with its
higher, "artificial" element swept away. Here and elsewhere he
reflects the "primordialist" fascination with human bestiality,
violence, and atavism which is notable among English and,
especially, American writers influenced by Darwinism. Jack
London's work is a prime example. The "call of the wild" is a
desire for self-immolation, a sinking of the cultured individual
identity in the emotive community of the herd or pack. This is
one of the many vicarious cults of a more "elemental" reality
which have arisen in industrial societies. Wells wrote one short
story for an American magazine in the crude primordialist mode.
"The Reconciliation" (1897) tells of a reunion of two friends who
have been estranged by sexual jealousy. From rational gestures of
friendship the meeting degenerates as the old jealousy is revived,
until one friend murders the other in a spasm of bestial hatred.
This is the material of pulp fiction, but elsewhere—in the panic
flight from London in The War of the Worlds, the reversion of the
Beast Men in The Island of Dr Moreau and the Battle of the Potwell

Inn in *Mr Polly*—Wells creates scenes of atavistic violence with a serious artistic purpose. Among these are his visions of future wars. In Wells's utopian visions, world unity is only achieved after a period of war and catastrophe. He repeatedly warned that the militant nation-states of Europe would end up by destroying one another, but he had no interest in complacent, liberal attempts to stabilise the situation or preserve a "balance of power". He was never a pacifist, and many of his admirers were repelled by his support of the First World War effort, although this gave way to disillusion when he saw that existing nation-states and ruling élites were going to be left intact. Social disintegration, an outbreak of the elemental, was a necessary prelude to reconstruction. The present social arrangements could only lead to disaster: but faced with an open and immediate choice between reversion and a fresh start, Wells hoped and believed that men would be shocked into compounding their differences. The Darwinist conception of the adaptation of the species leads to a curious association between the ideas of primitivism and progress. Both carry the suggestion of self-subordination, a sacrifice of individuality to the collective. The Victorian thinker, Herbert Spencer, held that matter evolves from a state of incoherent homogeneity to one of coherent heterogeneity; Wells saw human society as having attained to incoherent heterogeneity, and he sometimes seems to confuse the two ends of the evolutionary spectrum in his impatience with this middle. This is how he ended an article on "The Novels of Mr George Gissing" (1897):

> The clear change in the way of thinking that Mr.
> Gissing's Rolfe is formulating ... is no incidental change
> of one man's opinion, it is a change that is sweeping over
> the minds of thousands of educated men. It is the
> discovery of the insufficiency of the cultivated life and its
> necessary insincerities; it is a return to the essential, to
> honourable struggle as the epic factor in life, to children
> as the matter of morality and the sanction of the
> securities of civilisation.[24]

In the context, what seems to have been sweeping over thousands of educated minds in 1897 was a wave of imperialism. Wells's interpretation makes it a generalised rejection of liberal individualism. Morality should ensure the welfare of the children and of future generations, and not the fulfilment of individuals or the greatest present happiness of the greatest number. Men must "return to the essential"—to the collective experience of struggle —in order to go forward. In another book review written in 1897, he argued that a man's individuality is not his complete expression. "A man is a specimen of a species of social animal— plus a specimen of some sort of culture, plus a slight personal difference. If his culture has been sane, his desires, his emotions, his abiding happiness, lie in the good of the species—in the good of the generations to come."[25] This view of the individual and the species was restated many times. It is rigorously explored in one of the most bizarre projects Wells ever completed, the academic thesis which earned him a London University D.Sc. in 1944, at the age of 78. The argument is twofold: each individual is to be seen as a unique experiment conducted by the species, and the notion of integral and separate individuality, the atomistic self of liberal individualism, is a "biologically convenient delusion".[26] The delusion consists in an imputation of completeness and stable continuity to what is in fact "a collection of mutually replaceable individual systems held together in a common habitation".[27] Elsewhere Wells compares the individuality of the self to the uniqueness of particular atoms. Because of the disparity of scale we do not talk of cutting an atom with a knife or viewing it through a microscope; for the same reason, we assume all atoms to be uniform, and from a sufficiently detached perspective all men too are uniform.[28] Human consciousness can only admit this as an abstract proposition: but though men cannot experience the sense of homogeneity, they must cultivate the sense of coherence. Since the integrality of the self can be fragmented by analysis, it can also be subsumed in a synthesis. Wells argues in his doctoral thesis that the conditions under which the illusion of selfhood was biologically convenient no longer exist. Men now need to be less conscious of themselves as individuals, and more conscious of their membership of a species with a common, collective purpose.

Wells believed in the uniqueness of every unit of matter; and the shortcomings of his system would have appeared had he analysed the concept of "uniqueness" as carefully as he analyses "individuality". But though these ideas have their intrinsic interest, they have been discussed at length here because of their relation to his practise as a novelist. They are the "reconstruction of the frame", the scientific and philosophical inquiry which is presupposed everywhere in his imaginative work. As Van Wyck Brooks pointed out long ago,[29] his conception of the universe is characterised by "infinite plasticity", and this is reflected in the wealth of transformations of cosmic existence and material possibility, the aerobatic display of the human inventive spirit, in his scientific romances and stories. The individuals who figure in his social novels are also plastic. They do not seek maturity or self-fulfilment or go in search of their true identity, as George Eliot's heroines for example do. Wells was akin to D. H. Lawrence in rejecting what the latter called the "old stable ego" of character in the Victorian novel, though the technical means adopted by the two novelists were poles apart. Wells's heroes are instinctively fluid and free-ranging personalities, struggling in cramped surroundings to find social roles capacious enough for them to settle in comfortably. Their inner life is represented by their boyhood games and their adult fantasies and suffering. The violation and perversion of their individual plasticity by the constricting forms of society is the basis of Wells's humour and poignancy, and his moral stance as narrator is that of a curator of the innovations and mutations which, however premature in themselves, appear as the forerunners of a successful evolutionary development. In both romances and novels Wells's synthesising "species imagination", fusing a concern for creative individuality with a formulation of structures and relationships in a universal context, is the essential element. In his *Autobiography* he recalls how one day he and Conrad lay on the beach near Folkestone, discussing how they would describe a boat lying out in the water. Critics have overwhelmingly taken Conrad's side, but I find Wells's argument equally persuasive:

I said that in nineteen cases out of twenty I would just
let the boat be there in the commonest phrases
possible. Unless I wanted the boat to be important I would
not give it an outstanding phrase and if I wanted to
make it important then the phrase to use would depend
on the angle at which the boat became significant. . . . He
wanted to see it with a definite vividness of his own.
But I wanted to see it and to see it only in relation
to something else—a story, a thesis. And I suppose if I
had been pressed about it I would have betrayed a
disposition to link that story or thesis to something still
more extensive and that to something still more
extensive and so ultimately to link it up to my philosophy
and my world outlook.[30]

2

SCIENTIFIC ROMANCES:
THE ALTERNATING VISION

If we exclude the saga of Otto Noxious, "explorer and Mun-
chausen", reportedly written when he was seventeen,[1] Wells's
first scientific romance was a direct product of his South Kensington years. "The Chronic Argonauts" appeared as a serial in the
Science Schools Journal during 1888. As the title indicates, it is an
early version of *The Time Machine* told in a mannered and
euphemistic style which Wells later discarded. It contains a
mysterious scientist, an exposition of Time as the fourth dimension
and a brief journey into the past, and it makes an unfulfilled
promise to narrate a journey into the future. In the next six years
Wells wrote several more drafts, and his most famous future
vision gradually reached its permanent shape. *The Time Machine*
appeared as a serial and in book form in 1895, and attracted considerable attention, with one critic going so far as to call its author
a genius.[2] Quickened by this success, Wells wrote the bulk of his
scientific romances and short stories in the half-dozen fertile years
which followed. His popularity continued to grow, and it was
supplemented by the encouragement of fellow-artists like Conrad,
who wrote to him about *The Invisible Man*:

> I am always powerfully impressed by your work.
> Impressed is *the* word, O Realist of the Fantastic! whether
> you like it or not. And if you want to know what
> impresses me it is to see how you contrive to give over
> humanity into the clutches of the Impossible and yet
> manage to keep it down (or up) to its humanity, to its

flesh, blood, sorrow, folly. *That* is the achievement! In
this little book you do it with an appalling completeness.[3]

This is a representative comment, for Wells's assurance in domesti-
cating the Impossible has always been admired. The romances
are the work of a visionary with the acute observation and
descriptive power of a realistic novelist; and they show a remarkable skill in controlling the reader's response to fictitious science,
either by concealing the logical objections (to time-travelling, for
example), or more importantly by the startling revelation of the
deductive consequences of an idea. The story, "The Man who
could work Miracles", is a simple example: Mr Fotheringay, the
miracle-worker, stops the rotation of the globe in order to make
time stand still, and unwittingly starts a catastrophic hurricane as
everything above ground is jerked tangentially forward at five
hundred miles an hour. Or again, Wells's description in "The
New Accelerator" of life under a drug which speeds up the brain
(and therefore slows down the external world) is a triumph of
accuracy and deductive literalness, and the climax comes when he
reveals that his characters' movements are causing so much at-
mospheric friction that they are about to set themselves on fire.
These aspects of Wells's imagination have always led critics to
compare him to Jules Verne, and they are often seen as the twin
Founding Fathers of science fiction.[4] But in fact there are few
similarities between them. Most of Verne's well-known books
are adventure stories woven around some triumph of engineering,
the recognisable if distorted predecessor of a modern space rocket,
aeroplane or submarine. Wells is much freer with the laws of
nature, and his inventions are only briefly sketched, with the aim
of a pseudo-scientific plausibility rather than prediction. His
central interest was in Darwinism and the biological sciences, and
from them he drew a poetic and symbolic intensity of vision
which Verne never achieved (unless in *Journey to the Centre of the
Earth*), and which now appears as the true inheritance of the best
contemporary science fiction writers.

In 1923 Edward Shanks wrote that Wells's romances "are, in
their degree, myths; and Mr Wells is a myth-maker".[5] Bernard

Bergonzi substantiates this hint in *The Early H. G. Wells* (1961), the most valuable critical book yet to have appeared on Wells. He discusses *The Time Machine*, for example, as an "ironic myth". An alternative description of the romances which might come closer to Wells's own intentions and procedures would be "ideological fables". Both terms should be understood as implying that the romances are literary incarnations of a self-contained intellectual and imaginative universe corresponding to Wells's reconstruction of the "frame" of things as a thinker. Such an approach stresses the continuities underlying the exotic variety of particular shapes and settings to which Wells owes his reputation as a story-teller. His inventiveness, in fact, can be seen as the prolific transmutation of a small number of themes and structures. These may be shown in their earliest form by an analysis of *The Time Machine*.

Wells sends his Time Traveller out of human time—historical time—and into the cosmic time revealed by geology and astronomy. He travels forward into a future which is not only open but infinite, in order to discover the course of human evolution; and what he sees is humanity declining and eventually becoming extinct. The journey forward ends after thirty million years in a world in which organic life has regressed until it is indistinguishable from the rocks, and the earth is symbolically darkened by a solar eclipse. This chilling scene is a superb embodiment of the desolate and nihilistic intuitions of the age. Nineteenth-century industrial progress had been gained at the cost of the limitation and constriction of lower-class life which Wells himself knew; social Darwinists saw society as a jungle in which purposive human action gave place to "natural selection", and Positivists saw human nature as determined by laws of heredity and environment; increasingly during the 1880s and 1890s, experience and ideology combined to promote a deterministic or fatalistic attitude to individual destiny. Men are puppets at the mercy of social and cosmic forces; the idea constantly occurs in Wells, though it is usually presented only to be transcended. But in *The Time Machine* he reflected the pessimistic temper of social theory directly, creating in the future world a total image of a deter-

ministic society. The main body of the narrative is concerned with
one of the intermediate stages of the human future—the year
A.D. 802,701—and it is narrated at two levels. On the first, the
Traveller has a series of adventures which lead him into a partial
sympathy for the Eloi, the gay, childlike and insubstantial race
who occupy the earth's surface, and into fear and horror of the
sinister underground race of Morlocks. He becomes emotionally
attached to Weena, a timid Eloi girl he saves from drowning; and
he fights the Morlocks to get back the Time Machine, which they
have stolen. On the second level—which is equally prominent in
the story—he tries to understand and interpret this future society.
The narrative is shaped to the demands of scientific method; the
development of his experiences is integrated with the forming and
testing of social hypotheses. Four theories about the 802,701 world
are presented, with a considerable show of argument in each case.
At first, before the Time Traveller knows of the Morlocks, he
sees the Eloi as the decadent descendants of a civilisation which
attained complete control of the natural environment. In such
conditions, the struggle for existence would lapse, and qualities
of refinement and taste would be valued above intelligence,
physical strength, and mechanical and conceptual skill, so that the
race would pass the summit of progress and fall into inevitable
decline. The second theory extends this Darwinian reasoning to
cover the Morlocks. The two races are the descendants of Capital
and Labour respectively. The working classes have been confined
underground; the process was already beginning in the sub-
terranean workshops, the basements and the dark slums of nineteenth-century cities. The Morlocks—stumbling, pallid creatures
who are blinded by exposure to the sunlight—are the products of
half a million years of servility. But the Eloi find their inferiors so
repugnant that the Time Traveller changes his views again. The
Morlocks are the more vital race, condemned to remain underground until evolutionary modifications permit them to return
and conquer the surface. Finally there comes a gruesome realisation which overturns all the previous theories. The Morlocks are
engineers and meat-eaters; the leisured and ineffectual Eloi are
vegetarian. The Time Traveller at last understands that the people

to whom he is naturally drawn are simply the Morlocks' cattle.
By an inexorable development, they have changed in our eyes
from a happy, sunlit community of the free to a herd of weak and
terrified slaves. The Morlocks are shown as the superior race, but
they too are at the mercy of natural forces outside their control.
A remarkable passage describes their panic when the Time
Traveller accidentally starts a forest fire:

> "And now I was to see the most weird and horrible
> thing, I think, of all that I beheld in that future age.
> This whole space was as bright as day with the reflection
> of the fire. In the centre was a hillock or tumulus, sur-
> mounted by a scorched hawthorn. Beyond this
> was another arm of the burning forest, with yellow
> tongues already writhing from it, completely encircling
> the space with a fence of fire. Upon the hillside were some
> thirty or forty Morlocks, dazzled by the light and
> heat, and blundering hither and thither against each other
> in their bewilderment. At first I did not realise their
> blindness, and struck furiously at them with my bar, in a
> frenzy of fear, as they approached me, killing one and
> crippling several more. But when I had watched the
> gestures of one of them groping under the hawthorn
> against the red sky, and heard their moans, I was
> assured of their absolute helplessness and misery in the
> glare, and I struck no more of them. . . .
> "At last I sat down on the summit of the hillock, and
> watched this strange incredible company of blind things
> groping to and fro, and making uncanny noises to
> each other, as the glare of the fire beat on them. The
> coiling uprush of smoke streamed across the sky, and
> through the rare tatters of that red canopy, remote as
> though they belonged to another universe, shone the little
> stars. Two or three Morlocks came blundering into me,
> and I drove them off with blows of my fists, trembling as I
> did so. . . . Thrice I saw Morlocks put their heads down
> in a kind of agony and rush into the flames. But, at

last, above the subsiding red of the fire, above the
streaming masses of black smoke and the whitening and
blackening tree stumps, and the diminishing numbers
of these dim creatures, came the white light of the day."[6]

V. S. Pritchett acutely observed that "There are always fist-fights
and fires in the early Wells. Above all, there are fires."[7] Beyond
the fist-fights and the fires, one might add, there are the remote
and unattainable beacons of the "little stars". Wells's appeal to
the stars ("Till the earth is no more than a footstool"[8]) has been
described by A. L. Morton[9] as a kind of imaginative imperialism.
But that is to take his poetic symbolism too literally. An earlier
passage from *The Time Machine* illustrates some of the meanings
found in the stars in his romances:

> "Looking at these stars suddenly dwarfed my own
> troubles and all the gravities of terrestrial life. I thought of
> their unfathomable distance, and the slow inevitable
> drift of their movements out of the unknown past into the
> unknown future. I thought of the great precessional
> cycle that the pole of the earth describes. Only forty times
> had that silent revolution occurred during all the years
> that I had traversed. And during these few revolutions
> all the activity, all the traditions, the complex organisations,
> the nations, languages, literatures, aspirations, even the
> mere memory of Man as I knew him, had been swept
> out of existence. Instead were these frail creatures who had
> forgotten their high ancestry, and the white Things of
> which I went in terror."[10]

This passage, with its sudden juxtaposition of different scales of
time and space, presents the major effect of *The Time Machine* in
miniature. Nineteenth-century geology had established the vast
age of the earth and the short period of its human occupation. The
evidence had been bitterly disputed, and it implied a revolution in
human perspectives which Wells more than any other writer
was fitted to express. The deterministic and pessimistic cast of
The Time Machine corresponds to the sense of human belittlement

implicit in the scientific humanism of the period. But raising one's eyes from the mundane entanglement of fist-fights and fires to the stars has a dual effect. The stars may seem to offer shadowy emotional alternatives to earthbound frailty and fear; the human spirit can be affirmed and identified with the whole cosmic process.

No account of *The Time Machine* would be complete without mentioning the symbolism of the narrator himself. As he starts off on his machine the Time Traveller describes a liberating excitement, "a kind of hysterical exhilaration".[11] At the end, he has disappeared on another journey, and he becomes a representative of the unfettered, time-free human imagination, doomed by biology and history and yet able to move in it, to scan it and encompass it at will:

> One cannot choose but wonder. Will he ever return? It may be that he swept back into the past, and fell among the blood drinking, hairy savages of the Age of Unpolished Stone; into the abysses of the Cretaceous Sea; or among the grotesque saurians, the huge reptilian brutes of the Jurassic times. He may even now—if I may use the phrase—be wandering on some plesiosaurus-haunted Oolitic coral reef, or beside the lonely saline lakes of the Triassic Age. Or did he go forward, into one of the nearer ages, in which men are still men, but with the riddles of our own time answered and its wearisome problems solved? . . . He, I know—for the question had been discussed among us long before the Time Machine was made—thought but cheerlessly of the Advancement of Mankind, and saw in the growing pile of civilisation only a foolish heaping that must inevitably fall back upon and destroy its makers in the end. If that is so, it remains for us to live as though it were not so.[12]

Wells's scientific romances alternate the ideas of hope and despair, mastery and slavery, release and submission, and in doing so they reflect the opposing images of predetermined life and

utopian life which guide his social thought. In a perceptive essay,
Robert P. Weeks has described the structure of the "special
world" created in Wells's fiction:

> It is a world enclosed by a network of limitations and
> dominated by the image of a man driven by a profound
> and, at times, an irrational desire to escape. Although the
> network appears at first to be impenetrable, the
> hero finally succeeds in disentangling himself. This action
> invariably creates in him "a kind of hysterical exhilaration".
> But ultimately he experiences defeat in the form either of
> disillusionment or of death.[13]

A man breaking through the barriers; this is what can be loosely
called the Wellsian myth. We may go on to specify the means by
which Wells embodies the ideas of determinism and world
transformation in imaginative fables. The miracle of escape from
the known world into another world is accompanied by poetic
motifs such as pain, fire, an appeal to the stars, and the death-wish.
The consequent defeat is accomplished through an ironic reversal
such as the Time Traveller's discovery that the Morlocks are
masters and the Eloi are slaves. Wells's scientific romances, in fact,
are to be seen as explorations of a single imaginative universe.

Pain, fire, the death-wish, and the stars are all to be found in the
description of the forest fire in *The Time Machine*, quoted above.
When the Morlocks find themselves hemmed in and trapped by
the forces of nature, they rush to self-destruction, plunging "in a
kind of agony" into the flames. The only release here is to death,
but the passage may be compared with one from the other romance
Wells published in 1895, *The Wonderful Visit*. This story of an
angel's adventures in a Sussex village is a light-hearted and rather
trivial social satire. But at the end the angel plunges into a burning
house to rescue the servant-girl, Delia, the only person who has
responded to his "goodwill to all men", and the two are seen
ascending above the flames to heaven. Similarly (though this is to
anticipate) Mr Polly breaks out of his old life to begin anew after
setting his house on fire and trying unsuccessfully to commit
suicide.

39533

SUE BENNETT COLLEGE LIBRARY

Wells told an interviewer in 1899 that "In *The Wonderful Visit* I tried to suggest to people the littleness, the narrow horizon, of their ordinary lives by bringing into sharp contrast with typical characters a being who is free from the ordinary human limitations."[14] *The Invisible Man* (1897) was conceived on a similar pattern, but it gains a dramatic complexity through the struggle of a human protagonist—the scientific inventor Griffin—who tries to rise above the ordinary limitations. Wells achieves some memorable comic moments through the entanglements of Griffin with rustic types such as the tramp, Mr Thomas Marvel, and the villagers of Iping. In addition, although a slighter work than *The Time Machine*, *The Invisible Man* provides classic examples of Wells's use of world transformation motifs and ironic reversals. The transformation is enacted when Griffin describes how, after years of patient research, he at last took the drugs which were to make him invisible:

"But it was all horrible. I had not expected the suffering. A night of racking anguish, sickness, and fainting. I set my teeth, though my skin was presently afire, all my body afire, but I lay there like grim death. . . . I became insensible, and woke languid in the darkness.

"The pain had passed. I thought I was killing myself, and I did not care. I shall never forget that dawn, and the strange horror of seeing that my hands had become as clouded glass, and watching them grow clearer and thinner as the day went by, until at last I could see the sickly disorder of my room through them, though I closed my transparent eyelids. My limbs became glassy, the bones and arteries faded, vanished, and the little white nerves went last. I gritted my teeth and stayed there to the end. . . . At last only the dead tips of the fingernails remained, pallid and white, and the brown stain of some acid upon my fingers.

"I struggled up. At first I was as incapable as a swathed infant—stepping with limbs I could not see. I was weak and very hungry. I went and stared at nothing in

my shaving-glass—at nothing, save where an attenuated
pigment still remained behind the retina of my eyes,
fainter than mist. I had to hang on to the table and
press my forehead to the glass."[15]

Griffin's ordeal is succeeded by an intense elation, a spiritual
rebirth. He repays an old score by setting fire to his lodgings, and
goes out into the streets feeling "as a seeing man might do, with
padded feet and noiseless clothes, in a city of the blind".[16] (The
metaphor directs us to another of Wells's fables with a very similar
theme, "The Country of the Blind".) But Griffin's expectations
are swiftly overturned. Naked and unseen, he plunges into
Oxford Street, and immediately finds himself helpless amid the
bustling, hostile city crowd. People tread on his heels, hansom
cabs smash into him; the roads are rough underfoot and freezing
in the January weather, and his muddy footprints soon attract
attention. Griffin is forced to move from the city to the country,
but even in the sleepy Sussex village he becomes an unprotected
fugitive. His hasty temper leads him to retaliate with savage,
unprovoked assaults. He proclaims a "Reign of Terror", but his
ambition of dictatorship is short-lived, for he is tracked down and
killed. As he lies dead on the roadway, Wells unforgettably shows
the limitations of humanity reasserting themselves:

An old woman, peering under the arm of the big
navvy, screamed sharply. "Looky here!" she said, and
thrust out a wrinkled finger. And looking where
she pointed, everyone saw, faint and transparent, as though
made of glass, so that veins and arteries, and bones and
nerves could be distinguished, the outline of a hand—a
hand limp and prone. It grew clouded and opaque
even as they stared.
"Hallo!" cried the constable. "Here's his feet a-showing!"
And so, slowly, beginning at his hands and feet, and
creeping slowly along his limbs to the vital centres of his
body, that strange change to visible fleshliness continued.
It was like the slow spreading of a poison. First came
the little white veins tracing a hazy grey sketch of a

limb, then the glassy bones and intricate arteries,
then the flesh and skin, first a faint fogginess and then
growing rapidly dense and opaque. Presently they could
see his crushed chest and his shoulders, and the dim
outline of his drawn and battered features.[17]

This is a superbly ironic climax, but it is notable that, in spite of
the fright Griffin gives them, the forces of law and order eventually
triumph. A year earlier Wells had published *The Island of Dr
Moreau*, a romance with much more deeply horrifying implications. This is the story of a demonic scientist on a Pacific island
who tries to make animals into men by vivisective surgery. His
experiments fail, and instead the human characters—Dr Moreau
himself, his assistant Montgomery, and the castaway narrator,
Edward Prendick—are themselves inexorably forced back toward
the savage state. The story has often been read as allegory, and
Wells himself described it as a "theological grotesque".[18] Moreau
should be seen as parodying, not the orthodox Christian God, but
the hypothetical god or primal force behind the evolutionary
process as it was then seen—the "ethical process" or collective
drive from lower to higher forms of life.[19] To adopt Huxley's
image, Moreau is the governor which is overcome by the momen-
tum of the natural steam engine. He describes his life's work as the
"study of the plasticity of living forms"[20] and his outlook involves
the idea of pain as the symbol of slavery and limitation, the "mark
of the beast" which the evolution of the intellect has rendered
unnecessary. He passes his living victims through a "bath of
burning pain" in order that they may be freed of it. The cruelty
points to a savage contradiction between Moreau's ruthless figure
and the scientific, rationalist ideals which he represents in however
travestied a form. ("The plasticity of living forms", a phrase which
on Moreau's lips carries a peculiar *frisson*, was after all studied in a
sense by Darwin.) Anthony West, in an influential article, has
taken this contradiction as the basis for a psychological explanation
of Wells.[21] Accepting the pessimism of *The Time Machine* and
The Island of Dr Moreau as his deepest intuition, West sees his
later rationalistic optimism as a long exercise in self-repression.

This view has had its value as a corrective to earlier distortions, but the more closely Wells's best work is scrutinised, the more inextricably his optimism and his pessimism are found to be allied. It may be added that with a little ingenuity most satirists can be shown as cutting away the ground beneath their own feet. In some ways *The Island of Dr Moreau* resembles *Gulliver's Travels*, where the Houyhnhnms and the Yahoos present the critic with similar problems. This is not to deny that *Dr Moreau*, with the marriage of science and dictatorship in its central character, has as much right to the title of a prophecy as Wells's later works. But in addition to the repulsiveness of the things described, there is a set of values embodied in the narrator himself. Prendick is an isolated representative of "humanity", and he alone on the island shows the capacity for survival. At the beginning of the story he and two others are cast away on a boat, without provisions. He is the last of the three to yield to the temptation of cannibalism, and he manages to keep out of the fight which sends the other two overboard (these brutal incidents prepare the reader for the shocks to come). On the island he concludes wrongly that Moreau is experimenting on men, and that he is a chosen victim; so that his very humanity makes him a fugitive and hence the subject of the reader's fears. He lives through a series of transitions in which he is by turn hunter and hunted (these may have influenced Golding's *Lord of the Flies*), he sees Moreau and Montgomery bestialised and killed and their compound burnt down, and for months he is marooned on the island, one of a crowd of Beast Men reverting to bestiality. Somehow he preserves the human resourcefulness and dignity which Montgomery, Moreau, and his creations have lost. The cost is that of cutting himself off from ordinary humanity. The sailors who pick him up think him demented, and the England to which he returns seems like another land of Beast Folk who might at any time revert. He retires to an astronomical observatory, rather as Gulliver retires to his stables:

> My days I devote to reading and to experiments in chemistry, and I spend many of the clear nights in the study of astronomy. There is, though I do not know how

> there is or why there is, a sense of infinite peace and
> protection in the glittering hosts of heaven. There it must
> be, I think, in the vast and eternal laws of matter, and
> not in the daily cares and sins and troubles of men, that
> whatever is more than animal within us must find its
> solace and its hope.[22]

Prendick manages to survive and to point to the stars as the
direction in which humanity must aspire; but he has also learnt
to recognise the primitive savagery of ordinary human life,
particularly in cities, where "perfectly reasonable creatures, full
of human desires and tender solicitude" become in his eyes a
nauseating, threatening menagerie—"prowling women would
mew after me, furtive craving men glance jealously at me, weary
pale workers go coughing by me. . . . Then I would turn aside
into some chapel, and even there, such was my disturbance, it
seemed that the preacher gibbered Big Thinks even as the Ape
Man had done; or into some library, and there the intent faces
over the books seemed but patient creatures waiting for prey."[23]

The youthful exuberance of these passages is as notable as their
pungency. Wells was playing the melodramatic role of *enfant
terrible* assaulting the complacency of late Victorian society. Many
of his short stories are concerned, at varying levels of complexity
and seriousness, with the precariousness of man's supremacy and
the temporary nature of bourgeois order. There are more things
in heaven and earth than the reader dreams of. Runaway stars
come smashing through the solar system, men are attacked by
deep-sea creatures and giant orchids and spiders, the ants develop
a civilisation equal to man's. Stories like "The Empire of the
Ants", "The Sea Raiders", and "The Flowering of the Strange
Orchid" have had an immense progeny in later science fiction.
But the greatest and most influential story in this genre is Wells's
history of the Martian invasion of England, *The War of the
Worlds* (1898).

The War of the Worlds stands out among the scientific romances
as a triumph of realism. The topographical accuracy and vivid
observation of London and the home counties in the 1890s plays

an essential part in Wells's tense and absorbing description of the Martian tactics and the human panic. His narrative mastery here is clearly seen beside the comparatively vague and disembodied descriptions of war in his later romances *The Sleeper Awakes* and *The World Set Free*. In *Experiment in Autobiography* Wells records that in his early bicycling days he "wheeled about the (Woking) district marking down suitable places and people for destruction by my Martians",[24] and a future editor would do well to take up Bernard Bergonzi's suggestion that "one should read the opening chapters of *The War of the Worlds* with a map of West Surrey by one's side".[25] Yet for all this, Wells's Martian story is an ideological fable like his other romances. In portraying the insensibility of Suburban Man to danger, and the pathetic impotence of the military defences against the Martians' Black Smoke and Heat Ray, he takes a demonic pleasure in the overthrow of the self-styled master race. The narrative abounds with images which register the reversal of Victorian self-conceit. The Martian invasion is frequently compared with the brutal European colonisation of Tasmania, so that the agents of imperialist violence have now become its victims. In addition, there is a sustained rhetoric which interprets man's relation to the Martians through the relations of animals to man. They are doing to us, Wells points out, what we have done to monkeys, bison, dodos, cows, rabbits, rats or ants. The narrator speaks of "a sense of dethronement", a realisation that "the fear and empire of man had passed away".[26] After a few days the only means of resisting the Martians is "the preparation of mines and pitfalls"[27]—the method of our Stone Age ancestors. The humbling of man is completed when, in the most brilliant of Wells's ironic denouements, the release of the world is accomplished by the lowliest of terrestrial creatures, the micro-organic bacteria.

Various features of the story counteract this human ignominy. Once again there is a narrator possessing moral toughness and the will to survive. Another character, the Artilleryman, talks of assembling an élite band of men who will not tolerate subjection, and he confides a daydream of blazing, suicidal self-assertion in one of the Martians' Fighting Machines: "'Fancy having one of

them lovely things, with its Heat-Ray wide and free! Fancy
having it in control! What would it matter if you smashed to
smithereens at the end of the run, after a bust like that?'''.[28] The
Artilleryman is later shown up as a braggart and drunkard, but he
clearly points to the values which Wells himself invests in the
Martians. The narrator gives a minute description of the invaders
and their technology, and the result is a striking revelation of
Wells's ideals for humanity. The passage is enlivened by playful
allusions to his own article "The Man of the Year Million":

> It is worthy of remark that a certain speculative writer of
> quasi-scientific repute, writing long before the Martian
> invasion, did forecast for man a final structure not unlike
> the actual Martian condition. His prophecy, I remember,
> appeared in November or December, 1893, in a long
> defunct publication, the *Pall Mall Budget*, and I recall a
> caricature of it in a pre-Martian periodical called
> *Punch*. He pointed out—writing in a foolish facetious
> tone—that the perfection of mechanical appliances must
> ultimately supersede limbs, the perfection of chemical
> devices, digestion—that such organs as hair, external nose,
> teeth, ears, chin, were no longer essential parts of the
> human being, and that the tendency of natural
> selection would lie in the direction of their steady
> diminution through the coming ages. The brain alone
> remained a cardinal necessity. Only one other part
> of the body had a strong case for survival, and that was
> the hand, "teacher and agent of the brain". While
> the rest of the body dwindled, the hands would grow
> larger.
>   There is many a true word written in jest, and here in
> the Martians we have beyond dispute the actual
> accomplishment of such a suppression of the animal side
> of the organism by the intelligence.[29]

The narrator has earlier explained the reasons for this prodigious
evolutionary development and for the present invasion. The
Martians' own planet is cooling, and inhospitable conditions have

intensified their struggle for survival, while the warmer and
younger earth remains in a complacent torpor. In the future men
too will have to develop into "naked intelligences, things of new-
born wonder and thought" (the phrase comes from another
remarkable story, "Under the Knife"[30]) if they are to survive and
take control of their environment. Progress towards utopia means
the erosion of man's bestiality and the refinement of human
reason. This dream of the ascendancy of disembodied mind
reveals the dualistic character of Wells's thought, already evident
in "Human Evolution, an Artificial Process" with its distinction
between the inherited factor and the acquired factor in modern
man. Wells accepts the material and organic nature of mental
processes, and the distinction is not between mind and body, but
between different aspects of the mind. "Without the body the
brain would of course become a more selfish intelligence, without
any of the emotional substratum of the human being",[31] adds the
narrator in *The War of the Worlds*. This is both a statement of
the "ideological basis" of the story, and a veiled comment upon
it. Later romances like *A Modern Utopia* and *Men Like Gods* are
single-minded in their attitude to the achievement of disentanglement and control on another planet, but in *The War of the Worlds*
there is a careful ambiguity. The note on which the book ends—
the narrator's reunion with his wife—is a straight-forward and
conventional bow to the "emotional substratum". The ideas in
these early romances are not forcibly prescribed. Wells's great
power is one of astonishing the reader into participating in the
play of the speculative imagination.

The vision of a master civilisation organised on ruthlessly
rational lines is carried much farther in the last of his major
romances, *The First Men in the Moon* (1901). Like *The Time
Machine* this book combines an adventurous journey (by two
explorers, Bedford and Cavor) with the description of an alien
society. The journey to the moon and back is told by Bedford,
but the social analysis comes in the form of radio messages from
Cavor, who is left stranded among the Selenites. The implications
of this double-narrative structure will be discussed in the next
chapter. Cavor's dispatches, however, contain Wells's most

grotesque and fantastic vision of a society. Every citizen of the
moon is trained in childhood by a process of physical atrophy and
hypertrophy to fit a predetermined social function. The result is a
technocracy in which the idea of a rationalised human body is
carried to extravagant lengths. There are several kinds of intellectual workers, with brains distended in different ways; the
machine-minders have enormous hands, the glass-blowers "seem
mere lung-bellows", the news disseminators are "trumpet-
faced", the lunar police have overdeveloped muscles and servile
minds, and so on.[32] The moon is a world state ruled by the
egregious Grand Lunar, a vast braincase like an "opaque, feature-
less bladder".[33] Bernard Bergonzi, who rightly points out that
several features of Selenite society would elsewhere have drawn
Wells's approval, says that this monstrous and regal intelligence is
"no doubt meant to be impressive".[34] But this, it seems to me, is
controverted by the general tone of these chapters, again strongly
reminiscent of Swift. In 1902, before the serious quality of Wells's
romances was generally recognised, Arnold Bennett wrote of the
"powerful and sinister projection of the lunar world" as a "deeply
satiric comment upon this our earthly epoch of specialisation".[35]
Cavor, the narrator, does his ingenuous best to be fair to the
Selenites, but when he has divulged the secret of his spaceship he
is seized and killed. *The First Men in the Moon*, in fact, presents a
totalitarian state, in the tradition of Plato's Republic, so regulated
that it eliminates all freedom and spontaneous growth. Wells
attacks it with a two-way irony also aimed at the society of his
own day. The disturbing sight, for example, of rows of redundant
workers being kept drugged until new jobs are available for
them is followed by the reflexion that perhaps this is more humane
than condemning them to starve in the streets. The description of
the formation of young workers is even more caustic. Here Wells
is moving toward the mode of *Kipps* and *Mr Polly*, showing the
deterministic world at its most oppressive point, in the violation
and compression of the plastic young individual:

> "quite recently I came upon a number of young Selenites
> confined in jars from which only the fore-limbs protruded,

who were being compressed to become machine-minders of a special sort. The extended 'hand' in this highly developed system of technical education is stimulated by irritants and nourished by injection, while the rest of the body is starved. Phi-oo, unless I misunderstood him, explained that in the earlier stages these queer little creatures are apt to display signs of suffering in their various cramped situations, but they easily become indurated to their lot; and he took me on to where a number of flexible-minded messengers were being drawn out and broken in. It is quite unreasonable, I know, but such glimpses of the educational methods of these beings affect me disagreeably. I hope, however, that may pass off, and I may be able to see more of this aspect of their wonderful social order. That wretched-looking hand-tentacle sticking out of its jar seemed to have a sort of limp appeal for lost possibilities; it haunts me still, although, of course, it is really in the end a far more humane proceeding than our earthly method of leaving children to grow into human beings, and then making machines of them."[36]

As in *The Time Machine*, the cosmic journey of the moon ex-plorers leads only to the discovery of restriction and suppression. Yet once again their departure is accompanied by the Wellsian motifs of release and transcendence. They go to the moon in a sphere made of a special alloy, Cavorite, which overcomes gravity. The discovery of Cavorite is heralded by an explosion which wrecks its inventor's house, and the material itself is made by heating and cooling a mixture in a furnace. Bedford when travelling through space has a sense of "utter detachment and independence",[37] of a release from identity. At the end of the journey they arrive in a new world. Wells's description of this landing, with the lunar sunrise and the stirring of plant life, is one of his most powerful imaginative visions. In the imaginative universe of the romances, this is his myth of creation and resurrec-tion (the world of the Eloi in *The Time Machine* may also be

regarded as "paradisal" in nature[38]). There is a similar kind of
vision in *In the Days of the Comet* (1906), a book which holds an
uncertain position between the scientific romance and the social
novel. The early part of *In the Days of the Comet*, set in the Potter-
ies, binds together a love intrigue, industrial strife, and interna-
tional hostilities, working up towards a crescendo of melodrama.
As the emotional frenzy mounts a comet lights up the sky, coming
closer and closer to earth, until it discharges green vapours into
the atmosphere. With the vapours come oblivion and reawakening
in a fresh and transformed world. Freed of mental entanglements
by this passing star, the people of the earth destroy the structures
of the old life and begin the task of rebuilding. Though vivid at
times, this is a strained and inferior tale in which Wells indulges
but never quite exorcises his own relish for destruction. *The First
Men in the Moon*, however, also describes a freshly transformed
world, and here Wells unforgettably creates the miracle of new-
born life:

> How can I describe the thing I saw? It is so petty a
> thing to state, and yet it seemed so wonderful, so
> pregnant with emotion. I have said that amidst the stick-
> like litter were these rounded bodies, these little oval
> bodies that might have passed as very small pebbles. And
> now first one and then another had stirred, had rolled
> over and cracked, and down the crack of each of
> them showed a minute line of yellowish green, thrusting
> outward to meet the hot encouragement of the
> newly-risen sun. For a moment that was all, and then there
> stirred, and burst a third!
> "It is a seed," said Cavor. And then I heard him
> whisper very softly, "*Life!*".
> "Life!" And immediately it poured upon us that our
> vast journey had not been made in vain, that we
> had come to no arid waste of minerals, but to a world
> that lived and moved! We watched intensely. I remember
> I kept rubbing the glass before me with my sleeve, jealous
> of the faintest suspicion of mist.

The picture was clear and vivid only in the middle of
the field. All about that centre the dead fibres and
seeds were magnified and distorted by the curvature of the
glass. But we could see enough! One after another
all down the sunlit slope these miraculous little brown
bodies burst and gaped apart, like seed-pods, like the
husks of fruits; opened eager mouths that drank in the
heat and light pouring in a cascade from the newly-risen
sun.[39]

Imaginatively *The First Men in the Moon* is polarised between
grotesque satire and exploratory wonder, and both are realised in
visionary form, as scenes transmitted to the reader through the
cognitive activity of an observer. Wells's early romances make a
distinct group because they express an alternating vision, which
is structured upon opposing images rather than opposing actions.
The First Men in the Moon is a transitional work. It shows the
opposing images at their most vivid and at their most detachable.
The wonder and the satire are rather loosely related to one
another, and indeed the description of the lunar sunrise is slightly
flawed by an air of creating a self-conscious "purple patch". In a
less energetic writer this process might well have gone much
further, reducing an ideological juggling of images to a kind of
speculative aestheticism. But by 1901 the ebullient Wells was also
the author of *When the Sleeper Wakes*, *Love and Mr Lewisham*, and
Anticipations (a collection of sociological essays). Leaving a body
of classic science fiction behind him, he was making forays in
several new directions at once.

3

EXPLORER TO ACTOR

Throughout the vision of awakening plant life in *The First Men in the Moon*, the relative positions of observer and spectacle are never forgotten:

> Conceive it all lit by a blaze that would make the intensest sunlight of earth seem watery and weak. And still around this stirring jungle, wherever there was shadow, lingered banks of bluish snow. And to have the picture of our impression complete, you must bear in mind that we saw it all through a thick bent glass, distorting it as things are distorted by a lens, acute only in the centre of the picture, and very bright there, and towards the edges magnified and unreal.[1]

The two explorers watch from inside the Cavorite sphere, through the "thick bent glass" of windows whose curvature curiously resembles the curvature of a microscope. The narrator's attitude is much less that of the ostensible speaker—the obtuse prospector Bedford, who would hardly talk of an "arid waste of minerals"—than of Wells himself. The source of the sense of revelation which fills this passage is surely Wells's experience as a biology student. The microscopic mode of vision, which I believe to be implicit here, is the epitome of scientific observation or the disciplined study of images. As such, it has a particular imaginative importance in the scientific romances; another biological procedure, taxonomy, plays a comparable part in the social novels. Both methods have very distinct effects on the way in which objects are seen and understood. The opening paragraph of *The War of the Worlds* is a striking example of microscopic vision:

> No one would have believed, in the last years of the
> nineteenth century, that human affairs were being watched
> keenly and closely by intelligences greater than man's and
> yet as mortal as his own; that as men busied themselves
> about their affairs they were scrutinised and studied,
> perhaps almost as narrowly as a man with a microscope
> might scrutinise the transient creatures that swarm and
> multiply in a drop of water. With infinite complacency
> men went to and fro over this globe about their
> little affairs, serene in their assurance of their empire over
> matter. It is possible that the infusoria under the
> microscope do the same.[2]

When the globe is reduced to the size of a water-drop, humanity becomes an ant-like swarm and its affairs look contemptibly petty. The idea of man's "infinite complacency" then seems equally inevitable and equally objective. Wells insinuates the notion of a biology of human society, practised by godlike, superior beings, without the least awkwardness or fuss. In these masterly sentences the first of the Martians' blows to human prestige has already been dealt, and the reader is already on the defensive. The idea that we are being watched even as we watch the lower forms of life occurs again in some of Wells's most remarkable short stories, such as "The Star", "The Plattner Story", and "The Crystal Egg". The result is a double perspective on humanity, which may be illustrated by referring to another story, "In the Abyss". This tells of an inventor who descends in a steel bathysphere to the ocean floor. He returns to describe how mysterious creatures have captured the sphere and dragged it along the bottom towards a submarine city. They pull him through the streets and into a square where a vast congregation of their kind, apparently directed by a priest, starts chanting and bowing before him. After the inventor has escaped and told his tale, he makes a second descent from which he never returns. On one level "In the Abyss" is a simple and effective satire on religion, and in particular Christianity, with the unspoken imputation (perhaps) that the inventor has descended again only to be crucified. But behind this is the stranger idea of a material reality above and beyond terrestrial life which we could only know in the way that creatures on the ocean floor would know of our civilisation. As with the landing on the moon, the story is centred upon a vision seen through the windows of a sphere, and the roots of its imaginative distinction lie in the juxtaposition of the wonders of the deep sea with a vivid awareness of the difficulty and incompleteness of observation in the murky water. There is a similar juxtaposition when the Time Traveller tries to interpret the future, when the narrator of *The War of the Worlds* observes the Martians from his hideout in a ruined house, and when Wells interweaves a two-way irony into Cavor's sympathetic report on the Selenites. These early romances and stories are masterpieces of the exploratory or heuristic method, and they embody latent "double perspective" metaphors whenever they describe alien societies. The prose in many passages, including some of those quoted in the previous chapter, consciously pretends to the scientific virtues of clarity, precision, detachment, and an appropriate scepticism.

The idea of "social science" has been at the centre of one of the main intellectual debates of the last hundred years. Nineteenth-century Positivists claimed to be able to transfer the methods of the natural sciences wholesale into the study of human society. Wells, who followed the Pragmatist reaction against Positivism, held that scientific laws are not literal descriptions of the world but generalisations about discrete events whose differences are assumed to be of insignificant magnitude. Sociology cannot be an objective science because the observer cannot deal with humanity in sufficient numbers for the disparities of human consciousness and individuality to become insignificant. Instead, he argued in an essay on "The So-Called Science of Sociology",[3] it is a humanistic discipline working by persuasive argument rather than by experimental verification; the central sociological activity ought to be utopography, or the projection and criticism of ideal societies. But in spite of this rebuttal, the idea of a science of society fascinated Wells, and many of his imaginative attitudes at least are not alien to the spirit of modern empirical sociology. A scientific knowledge of humanity is one of his symbols for the attainment of mastery over nature. Such mastery is often emulated by his narrative attitude to his human material; one effect of this was described by Conrad, when he told Wells that "There is a cold jocular ferocity about the handling of that mankind in which you believe, that gives me the shudders sometimes".[4] But this detachment is only preserved to the end in some of the short stories (Conrad was referring to "Filmer", the story of a frightened aviator). In the romances the narrator-explorer is invariably drawn into some sort of relation with the alien community he is observing. His personal sympathies become involved, or the individuals he observes become too distinctive to fit his categories. He is imaginatively identified with the aliens in some way, or he moves right onto the stage and becomes an actor in their social drama. The element of involvement becomes increasingly important in Wells's work, eventually bringing with it the more excitable and impressionistic prose of the adventure story (as in *The Food of the Gods* and *The War in the Air*).

In *The Time Machine* Wells hints at the most hackneyed of all "involvement" devices, that of a love-affair between explorer and alien. Later, however, he used the more supple technique of channelling off some of the revulsion inspired by Beast Men, Martians or Selenites and directing it against subsidiary human figures in the story. Prendick in *The Island of Dr Moreau* vents his contempt on the drunken, feckless Montgomery. The narrator in *The War of the Worlds* is capable of a ruthless disregard of other people, which is intended to demonstrate his "fitness to survive" in unexpectedly hostile conditions. This is most clearly seen in his relationship with the Curate, another fugitive with whom he is trapped for several days in a house at Mortlake. The narrator spends his time making scientific observations of the Martians; the Curate whines about his soul and steals his companion's rations. In the end the Curate becomes deranged, and the narrator clubs him and leaves him to be captured by the Martians. In the interest of self-preservation he had no choice, and he feels his action will be approved by all who have not escaped the "dark and terrible aspects of life".[5] Certainly it would be approved by the "selfish intelligence" of the Martians. The narrator is a scientist, a pure mind aspiring to the Martian state of disembodiment; the Curate is a sensualist, a slave to his animal passions. The narrator's allegiance is divided between loyalty and disdain for humanity, and through this Wells skilfully insinuates a sympathy for the Martians which prepares for the haunting emotional depth of the novel's climax, when any feeling of chauvinistic triumph is overlaid by the poignant defeat of the genuine master race.

The contrast of the narrator and the Curate, the scientist and the sensualist (Orwell's "scientific man" and "romantic man") appears again and again in Wells, with the same mutual wariness and contempt, and the same more or less unsatisfactory partisanship on their author's part. The more successful treatments of the theme include *Men like Gods* (with its caricature of Churchill trying to plant the Union Jack in Utopia), *Tono-Bungay* (George and Edward Ponderevo) and the contrast of Bedford and Cavor in *The First Men in the Moon*. These two are a very ill-matched pair of explorers, and as each takes his turn as narrator, the result might appear to be a disjointed book, with the Swiftian final chapters strung on to the preceding adventures as an afterthought. But, in fact, the two accounts are deliberately complementary, and grow out of the difference between the two men. When they are arrested by the Selenites, Cavor wants to go down with them to the moon's interior, and anticipates a courteous reception. Bedford's only thought is to escape—he expects "guns, bombs, terrestrial torpedoes"[6] to be used against them—and to return to the moon, armed, in order to establish a gold-mining concession by force. Later, Cavor's radio messages to earth repeat the whole story of the moon journey, but they do not duplicate Bedford's account because Cavor's interest is in scientific observation rather than in the impressionistic rendering of adventures. Bedford edits Cavor's account, and there is an amusing interplay between the two types:

> "Poor Bedford," he says of me, and "this poor young man"; and he blames himself for inducing a young man, "by no means well equipped for such adventures," to

> leave a planet "on which he was indisputably fitted
> to succeed" on so precarious a mission. I think he
> underrates the part my energy and practical capacity played
> in bringing about the realisation of his theoretical sphere.[7]

The scientific impartiality of the narrator gives place here to the
artistic impartiality of an author deploying his characters. Bedford
and Cavor almost become the actors in a farcical sub-plot, and
Wells, in general, attached too much weight to the opposition of
scientist and sensualist to allow him to repeat this. In his later
works the opposition reappears in many individual forms, and
among these two broad tendencies may be distinguished. In the
first, the clash of scientific and sensual qualities is dramatised as an
internal, psychological conflict; in the second, it is seen as a social
conflict. Either way, the story enters the realm of lived experience
which an observer can only know by induction.

"The Moth" and "Pollock and the Porroh Man" are early
stories of men destroyed by psychic obsession, but they have little
of Wells's distinctive genius, and the second of them is clearly
indebted to Kipling. *The New Machiavelli* (1911) has for its theme
the conflict of constructive political ambition and sexual passion,
and will be discussed later; "A Dream of Armageddon" is a
preliminary sketch of this theme set in a society of the future, and
The Sea Lady (1902) repeats the same situation in a romantic and
lightweight form. But the finest of these psychological studies is
that of yet another rising politician, Lionel Wallace, in "The Door
in the Wall". To outward appearance Wallace is a man of
growing eminence who is about to take a seat in the Cabinet.
But he is obsessed by the memory of a small door through which
as a boy he once strayed into an enchanted garden, a world of
perpetual childhood and happiness. The vision of the door has
returned to him from time to time, but always at moments of
particular entanglement in worldly affairs—when he is late for
school, or travelling up to Oxford for his scholarship, or rushing
to the House of Commons to vote in a crucial division. As his
career approaches fulfilment, he confides to a friend that his
obsession is becoming intolerable. A few months afterwards, he

is found dead at the bottom of a deep shaft on a building site, to which access is gained by a small door in a wall.

In Wallace, a rational, worldly ambition is overcome by regressive self-indulgence. He has abandoned the struggles of mankind for an image of immortal and static satisfaction. The slightly mawkish sensuality of the enchanted garden is well brought out by Bernard Bergonzi, who points to the Freudian implications, and adds that the Wordsworthian myth of childhood is also present.[8] In the grey everyday world of the London streets in which Wallace vainly searches for his door, there is a sense of "shades of the prison-house" closing on the growing boy. On his early visit to the garden, a "sombre dark woman"[9] shows him a book containing his life up to the moment when he hesitated before the door. He hastily turns to the next page, and the garden around him vanishes; his brief escape from the determinism of time is over. The eventual coincidence of release and death links "The Door in the Wall" to the scientific romances, but the primordial, sensual image of the enchanted garden suggests a difference, which will later emerge in *Mr Polly*, between Wells's imaginative conceptions of individual transfiguration and of social transformation.

"The Door in the Wall" appeared in 1906, and its theme of individual release connects it with Wells's social comedies. Meanwhile, he had been writing a very different series of works, the romances beginning with *The Sleeper Awakes* (originally published as *When the Sleeper Wakes*, 1899). I have suggested that these are separated from the earlier romances by their active presentation of social experience. Wells himself saw the difference in other terms:

> (*The Sleeper Awakes*) is the first of a series of books which
> I have written at intervals since (1898); *The World
> Set Free* is the latest; they are all "fantasies of possibility";
> each one takes some great creative tendency, or group of
> tendencies, and develops its possible consequences in
> the future. . . . "Suppose these forces to go on," that
> is the fundamental hypothesis of the story.[10]

In the "fantasy of possibility" Wells was adopting aims rather like those of Jules Verne, except that he was interested in predicting social rather than technical developments. As a result these stories ("A Story of the Days to Come" and *The War in the Air* as well as those already named) are conceived as quasi-realistic novels of the future, without the imaginative licence of the earlier romances. Wells did not include *The Food of the Gods* or *In the Days of the Comet* in his definition, but these might be called "allegories of possibility" since their prediction of social change is not direct but oblique. *The Food of the Gods* (1904) describes the discovery of Boomfood, a substance which stimulates growth and produces a family of human giants who are restricted and persecuted by their fellow-citizens. Wells later pointed out that the story represents the conflict of large-scale and small-scale forms of human organisa-tion, and connected it with a Fabian talk he had given on the size of administrative areas.[11] But in spite of vivid moments, it is a crude and unwieldy allegory. *In the Days of the Comet* (1906) symbolises human revolution by showing the aftermath of a cosmic accident. It is presented as the autobiography of a man of the future, Leadford, looking back over his life before and after the "Change". The early part contains Wells's only fictional portrayal of the industrial conflict of his day. The confused violence of the people, their material deprivations, and Leadford's own emotional tumult are inextricably mixed, and together they create a strong image of the feverishness of pre-revolutionary life. But the pretence of narrative superiority, of a sane retrospective understanding made possible by the green vapours of the comet, is never convincingly established. Leadford's precipitate actions make him an outcast, and he claims his experience as socially "representative", standing for "all the disinherited of the world":[12] but this is self-dramatisation rather than objective analysis. Wells's failure to impersonate the imaginative transcendence at which he aimed is evident in the strained and lurid quality of the novel. His later work never wholly succeeds in purging a single-minded, scientific vision of its bestial and sensual elements.

Wells's actual "fantasies" of possibility include some which remain interesting only for the predictions they make, such as "The Land Ironclads" with its forecast of the tank, and *The*

World Set Free (1914) with its nuclear war set in the late 1950s. At their best, however, the fantasies contain a hero who, like Leadford, is both explorer and actor, and who genuinely elicits and concentrates the social experience of his community. In *The Sleeper Awakes* the dramatic and heuristic methods are rather clumsily mixed. This book projects forward the monopolistic economic tendencies of Wells's day to show a "nightmare of Capitalism triumphant",[13] two hundred years ahead. It presents an image of the future city, with its masses of underground workers, brutal police force, communal dining rooms, blaring advertisements and artificial climate, which recurs time after time in later science fiction.[14] Into this world awakes Graham, a nineteenth-century man who has spent the intervening time in a trance (a device Wells borrowed from Edward Bellamy's famous utopia, *Looking Backwards*, 1888). During his sleep Graham's investments have accumulated to such an extent that he has become nominal Owner of the World, and the trustees of his estate are the autocratic rulers. As in *The Time Machine*, the gulf between the classes has greatly widened, and among the enslaved common people Graham is a legendary hero who will one day lead a revolutionary uprising. He takes part in a revolt led by the opportunist politician, Ostrog, who manipulates the popular agitation for his own ends, and then opposes him in the name of democracy. The book ends with him facing Ostrog's forces in single aerial combat, while the masses cheer from below. Wells was not a great believer in popular democracy, and few of his books show such a straightforward allegiance with the oppressed and exploited. As Bernard Bergonzi points out,[15] Ostrog's tough-minded élitism is closer to Wells's usual position; J. Kagarlitski adds that Graham, on his side, propounds a kind of Christian Socialism.[16] Behind the opposing political rhetorics, however, there is a deeper problem, which George Orwell pointed to when he wrote that "Those armies of underground workers, with their blue uniforms and their debased, half-human language, are only put in 'to make your flesh creep'".[17] Graham learns about the future world through his own observations and through informants, and he is immediately drawn into political action, so that the narrative is an unsatisfactory mixture of social survey and adventure story. The underground armies are observed and reported on, and the effect is very like that of a television documentary. When Graham becomes their leader, he is still a lone individual, excelling as a broadcaster and fighter pilot, with the shouting, surging mob behind and beneath him. His real struggle is for publicity and the assertion of his own histrionic power. It is plain from *Anticipations* (1901) that Wells expected mass democracy to decline into this sort of baseless demagogy, as indeed it often has done. But *The Sleeper Awakes* is a shrewd, sensational scare-story rather than a searching analysis of the coming capitalist nightmare.

"A Story of the Days to Come" appeared shortly after *The Sleeper* in 1899, and it portrays the same future London under conditions of political stability. The major departure in this rather neglected story is the adoption of a hero who is an ordinary citizen of the future. Although Wells abandons the alien observer, he introduces a historical and cultural perspective in a novel way. "A Story of the Days to Come" is one of a pair of stories with close structural affinities; the other is "A Story of the Stone Age". Each is centred around a pair of lovers. Initially the man has to win the woman by outwitting a powerful rival, and the pair suffer physical exile and social displacement as a consequence. A number of dangers must then be overcome, one of which is the continued enmity of the rival in a disguised form. Finally, the lovers return and inherit the rival's position. The geographical setting of each story is London and western Surrey, and the other parallels include an explicit reference back to "The Stone Age" in "The Days to Come". "The Stone Age", which sets the events outlined in a paleolithic tribal context, is of no great literary interest, except in so far as it provides the themes for "The Days to Come": the conflict between the bestial nature of man and the precarious civilising process, and the investigation of the degree of human progress separating the "Epoch of Great Cities" from the "Age of Unpolished Stone".

In the world of "The Days to Come" there is once again a total separation of classes and cultures; the middle class have become

effete and fastidious, and the working class are stunted and brutal-
ised. Bourgeois "refinement" is caricatured at the beginning of the
story, with the hypnotic inducement of escapist dreams, the
wearing of pneumatic clothes to suggest enormous muscles (both
of which may be pointedly compared with the conditions of life
in "The Stone Age") and the anaemic breakfast of the future:

> It was a very different meal from a Victorian breakfast.
> The rude masses of bread needing to be carved and
> smeared over with animal fat before they could be made
> palatable, the still recognisable fragments of recently
> killed animals, hideously charred and hacked, the eggs torn
> ruthlessly from beneath some protesting hen—such things
> as these, though they constituted the ordinary fare
> of Victorian times, would have awakened only horror and
> disgust in the refined minds of the people of these
> latter days. Instead were pastes and cakes of agreeable and
> variegated design, without any suggestion in colour or
> form of the unfortunate animals from which their
> substance and juices were derived. They appeared on little
> dishes sliding out upon a rail from a little box at one side
> of the table.[18]

Wells's impersonation of the twenty-first century attitude creates
a two-way irony here: since their "pastes and cakes" are still
derived from the same "unfortunate animals", their "refinement"
is seen to consist only in shutting the mind to unpleasant facts.
The bloodless quality of middle-class existence is revealed in a
phrase like "agreeable and variegated design". In this setting, the
lovers, Elizabeth and Denton, are separated by parental edict,
and Elizabeth is brainwashed by hypnosis. When they are re-
united, the struggle for subsistence leads them first to venture out
into the desolate countryside, where they are savaged by wild
dogs, and then to put on the blue canvas of the labour serfs and
go to work in the underground machine-shops. The workers are
shown both as victims of the capitalists and the Labour Company
or workhouse system, and as the representatives of a permanent
bestiality in the human race; they are condemned to a barbarity

which has persisted since the Stone Age. Denton has to learn to
accept his fellowship with these people, and to defend himself in
their constant fights. The element of recoil here (as with the Eloi
and the Morlocks), suggests that Wells, coming from the lower-
middle class, was not immune to the more hysterical nineteenth-
century fears of working-class brutishness; but at the same time
the people of the underways are much more individualised than
in *The Sleeper Awakes*. The descriptions have a crude power and
a primordialist rhetoric later found in Jack London. Denton's
middle-class refinement is filed down by involvement, until he
becomes a representative figure of human integrity, caught
between the forces of civilised fraud and bestial anarchy, and
articulating the whole experience of his fellow-citizens:

> Denton went home, to fall asleep exhausted and wake in
> the small hours with aching limbs and all his bruises
> tingling. Was it worth while that he should go on living?
> He listened to Elizabeth's breathing, and remembering
> that he must have awaked her the previous night, he
> lay very still. He was sick with infinite disgust at the new
> conditions of his life. He hated it all, hated even the
> genial savage who had protected him so generously. The
> monstrous fraud of civilisation glared stark before his
> eyes; he saw it as a vast lunatic growth, producing a
> deepening torrent of savagery below, and above ever
> more flimsy gentility and silly wastefulness.[19]

Though he is closer to the texture of life than Graham, Denton's
stand against sensuality and disorder still has a cardboard, histrionic aspect:

> He began to rave and curse at the intolerable forces which
> pressed upon him, at all the accidents and hot desires
> and heedlessness that mock the life of man. His little voice
> rose in that little room, and he shook his fist, this
> animalcule of the earth, at all that environed him about,
> at the millions about him, at his past and future and all
> the insensate vastness of the overwhelming city.[20]

Denton invokes this cosmic determinism in order to rationalise his private despair, and his railing against fate gives place to cautious moralising about the immense slowness of the evolutionary process when he is returned to the middle class by an unexpected legacy. But the individual experiencing social outrage is something very different from the speculative determinism of the early romances, and despite faults of inadequate characterisation and over-elaborate plotting, "The Days to Come" is an important stage in Wells's emergence as a social novelist.

The War in the Air (1908) suggests even more firmly that Wells's creative interests had swung over to the social novel. It is mainly remembered, perhaps, for its vision of the vast Zeppelin fleet hanging over New York. But the opening chapter, with its more subtle portrayal of the impingement of technical progress on ordinary life, is a small masterpiece of comic generalisation. Wells's sureness in seizing the instantly evocative detail from the maze of contemporary phenomena is brilliantly exemplified:

> "He's a go-ahead chap, is Bert," said Tom. "He knows a thing or two."
>
> "Let's hope he don't know too much," said Jessica, who had a fine sense of limitations.
>
> "It's go-ahead Times," said Tom. "Noo petaters, and English at that; we'll be having 'em in March if things go on as they do go. I never see such Times. See his tie last night?"[21]

> (Bert's motor-cycle) was a sturdy piece of apparatus, and it had acquired a kind of documentary value in these quick-changing times; it was now nearly eight years old.[22]

The chapter is founded upon the contrast of the Smallways brothers. Tom, rooted to the earth and only concerned about technological marvels when they drop ballast on his potatoes, is the remnant of a static society. Bert's is a "progressive" temperament, impressionable and flashy. Both are the victims of runaway social change. Bert is blown haphazardly over the world—his flight in a balloon he cannot navigate sums up his life—while Tom endures at home, and after thirty years of destruction comes out rather better than Bert in a world where social order has given way to the immemorial subsistence of peasant communities. Tom's pithy remarks circumscribe the whole civilised madness of the book, so that the experience of helplessness is conveyed through the pastoral convention of rustic wisdom:

> "This here Progress," said Mr. Tom Smallways, "it keeps on."
> "You'd hardly think it *could* keep on," said Mr. Tom Smallways.[23]

And lastly:

> "You can say what you like," he said. "It didn't ought ever to 'ave begun."
> He said it simply—somebody somewhere ought to have stopped something, but who or how or why were all beyond his ken.[24]

There is a final emphasis upon the gap between Wells and his character, for though the technological pessimism is shared and sums up the book, Wells is insinuating that he himself has plenty of ideas about the "who or how or why", and that his analyses can be found elsewhere—in his political books, *Anticipations* (1901) and *New Worlds for Old* (1908), for instance. But the rustic wisdom remains valid, for *The War in the Air* betrays little confidence that somebody somewhere will call the arms race to a halt. Of all the romances it is the most closely engaged with the contemporary world. As Wells narrowed his gaze from the reconstruction of the frame of the universe to the society and the individualities he knew, the exhilarating, godlike human qualities and their imagined outcome—release from the determined world to a transformed world—were lost sight of. All the "fantasies of possibility" are transitional in character, and *The War in the Air* can be seen as an act of submission, a temporary abandonment of the rational, scientific dream of release and control, in which the only positive value is that of native human stoicism. In turning to the social novel Wells was forced to remake the connexions between his optimism and his pessimism.

4

THE COMEDY OF LIMITATION

There is little doubt that Wells thought of the novel as a more challenging form than the romance. The publication of *Love and Mr Lewisham* (1900) was greeted, predictably enough, with the suggestion that he had strayed beyond the limits of his talent.[1] "I *will* write novels", he protested to Arnold Bennett; his romances were the freaks of inspiration, but novels were "the proper stuff for my everday work, a methodical careful distillation of one's thoughts and sentiments and experiences and impressions".[2] Both *Love and Mr Lewisham* and *Kipps* were the products of constant revision. As Gordon N. Ray has demonstrated in his important study "H. G. Wells Tries to be a Novelist" (1960), Wells at the start of the century was determined to excel at what he had called, in one of a forthright and discriminating series of fiction reviews, "the most vital and typical art of this country and period".[3] Yet the first fruits of his determination were the social comedies—works which have been abundantly loved for their warmth, gaiety, and anarchic humour, but which have only too rarely engaged the attention of literary critics. Henry James's ambivalent response to *Kipps*—"not so much a masterpiece as a mere born gem"[4]—can be taken as expressing the general opinion. It is true that there is a yawning gap in *Love and Mr Lewisham*, at least, between the slightness and unevenness of Wells's achievement, and the artistic ambitions which he later recalled: "It was consciously a work of art; it was designed to be very clear, simple, graceful, and human."[5] But these terms are fitting enough when we come to the finest of the comedies, *The History of Mr Polly* (1910). Here at last Wells wrote a vital, enduring novel, infused with a sophisticated art beneath the intuitive surface.

In all his early novels Wells combines the detachment of comedy with a penetrating study of individual development. In *Love and Mr Lewisham* the mixture is not a happy one. At first the hero is repeatedly called "Mr Lewisham", and the narrative is arch and mannered; by the end he is invariably "he", and he has become a mouthpiece for Wells's ideas and attitudes. Lewisham is a poor but gifted science student whose experiences are fairly close to Wells's own. The result, however unsatisfactory, is at least a novel in which—as Bernard Shaw wrote of his novel, *The Irrational Knot*—"the morality is original and not readymade". Lewisham's life becomes a choice between a career of possible intellectual attainments and the acceptance of undistinguished drudgery in support of a wife and family. His promise as a student fades as he develops a sexual fixation for his narrow, conventional girl-friend Ethel. He marries her and subdues himself, later reproaching himself bitterly for the sacrifice of his ambitions. But this is only adolescent self-pity; maturity comes through the tutelage of his dubious father-in-law, the spiritualist medium Chaffery, who writes to him at his lowest point that "you are having a very good time, you know, fighting the world".[6] Lewisham at last fully embraces the day-to-day role of father and breadwinner of a family. The final chapter is entitled "The Crowning Victory"; he tears up the "Schema" or programme of his ambitions which had guided the sterile fact-grubbing of his scholastic years, and turns instead to his child. It is not that domesticity brings a sense of comfortable fulfilment. The ideal of self-fulfilment is connected with the vanity of his career, and in rejecting this Lewisham at last goes beyond himself, dedicating himself to the general evolutionary struggle of humanity. The story began with him living in an attic filled with timetables, certificates, and admonitory slogans. Stuffy, angular, and unventilated, the attic is a perfect image of his mind; its physical shape, with "lead-framed dormer windows, a slanting ceiling and a bulging wall",[7] even bears a shadowy resemblance to his bespectacled face. The view from the windows, and the stirring

spring weather outside, are the main threat to his regulated cramming. At the end, however, he is seen in a room described solely
in terms of its "spacious outlook" over the bustle of Clapham
Junction. His loyalty is now to the dynamic process of life itself.
There is an interesting contrast with the ending of Arnold Bennett's first novel, *A Man from the North* (1898), which may be
brought out by brief quotations:

> He heard the trot of the child behind him. Children . . .
> Perhaps a child of his might give sign of literary ability.
> If so—and surely these instincts descended, were not
> lost—how he would foster and encourage it! (Bennett).[8]

> "Come to think, it is all the Child. The future is the
> Child. The Future. What are we—any of us—but
> servants or traitors to that? . . ." (Wells).[9]

Bennett's failed writer is simply finding consolation in defeat;
Lewisham does not postpone the quest but rejects personal
ambition altogether. Wells here is dramatising the ethical premise
of his biological humanism—a man's individuality is not his
complete expression—and the result is somewhat forced and
didactic. The same beliefs are voiced much more vividly by
Chaffery, the demonic *raisonneur* of the novel, under the pretext
of a discussion of spiritualism. Full of virtuous indignation,
Lewisham has come to denounce his father-in-law's mediumistic
frauds. Chaffery welcomes him volubly, and argues that he is a
much more consistent socialist than Lewisham, since he cheats the
rich rather than deceiving himself. He goes on to attack the
naïvely phenomenal approach of South Kensington science, and
to overwhelm his listener with philosophical puzzles:

> "I sometimes think with Bishop Berkeley, that all
> experience is probably something quite different from
> reality. That consciousness is *essentially* hallucination. I
> here, and you, and our talk—it is all Illusion. Bring your
> Science to bear—what am I? A cloudy multitude of
> atoms, an infinite interplay of little cells. Is this hand
> that I hold out, me? This head? Is the surface of my skin

any more than a rude average boundary? You say it
is my mind that is me? But consider the war of
motives. Suppose I have an impulse that I resist—it is
I resist it—the impulse is outside me, eh? But suppose that
impulse carries me and I do the thing—that impulse is
part of me, is it not? Ah! My brain reels at these mysteries!
Lord! what flimsy fluctuating things we are—first this,
then that, a thought, an impulse, a deed and a forgetting,
and all the time madly cocksure we are ourselves."[10]

Lewisham's whole internal development is a "war of motives".
He is "madly cocksure" in the argument about spiritualism, and
"madly cocksure" in his intellectual ambitions, and he has to
learn to see himself as a "flimsy fluctuating thing" in a larger
social and natural process. In spite of his rhetorical appeal to the
future, he comes to adopt an excessively defeatist attitude. The
bare ideals of survival and persistence belong much more properly
in the bleak world of *The War in the Air*; Wells later wrote that
the submissiveness of *Love and Mr Lewisham* betrayed incipient
"domestic claustrophobia"[11] in himself. Certainly some timid
special pleading was needed to justify Lewisham's parting from
the blue-stocking girl who is his last link with the upper world
of careerism and success:

"The thing is, I must simplify my life. I shall do nothing
unless I simplify my life. Only people who are well off
can be—complex. It is one thing or the other—"[12]

Gordon N. Ray points out that the feeling here is echoed in one
of Wells's newspaper pieces, a transparent exercise in mock-
renunciation called "Excelsior":

Better a little grocery, a life of sordid anxiety, love, and a
tumult of children, than this Dead Sea fruit of success.
It is fun to struggle, but tragedy to win.[13]

Lewisham is deliberately sent down into this limited, lower-class
world. Wells was both deeply aware of the divisiveness of
Victorian class consciousness, and divided himself in his attitude

to the world he had left. The conflict could not be resolved through an articulate, naturally complex figure like Lewisham; Wells may have been in a similar position to Lewisham in the obscure years of his first marriage (1891–3), but he did not submit to "simplicity" for long. In his other social novels lower-class life takes a more sinister aspect. In *The Wonderful Visit* the villagers are said to be "pithed" in their formative years, so that they accept their allotted stations;[14] and the spectre of the manipulative and compressive education of the Selenites stands behind the portrayal of individual development in *Kipps* and *Mr Polly*. Polly is compared to a rabbit in a trap, and one of Kipps's fellow-apprentices declares bitterly: "we're in a blessed drain-pipe, and we've got to crawl along it till we die".[15] In these books the experience of the simple hero, the "little man" confined in the nets of the retail trade, is revealed and interpreted by a complex narrator addressing the reader from what Wells elsewhere called "our educated standpoint".[16] This interplay of narrator and character leads to an alternation of worlds similar to that in the scientific romances. The two images of deterministic and utopian life are now seen against the class structure of English society. The comedy arises from a confrontation between the class into which Wells was born and the class into which he adventured, and it leads towards a new world of escape from the limitations of either.

The first and least substantial of his comic heroes is Hoopdriver, the draper's assistant in *The Wheels of Chance* (1896). This "Holiday Adventure" is constructed around a cycling tour of southern England. Hoopdriver, enjoying his annual ten days of freedom, is released into an idyllic world where class distinctions temporarily disappear, and he becomes involved in a fragile and sentimental intrigue with a middle-class girl. *The Wheels of Chance* has a period charm, as a record of the home counties undisturbed by the motor-car, but its high spirits are deadened by the facetiousness of the prose style which Wells had developed for his humorous sketches in the *Pall Mall Gazette*. (*Certain Personal Matters* is a representative selection of these.) The humour is choked by the assumptions of respectability; writer and reader are assumed to

be familiar only with the customer's side of the counter, and Wells
is torn between the impulse to express Hoopdriver's experience
and the impulse to disown all kinship with him. During 1903–4,
he returned to *The Wheels of Chance* and produced a dramatised
version, entitled *Hoopdriver's Holiday*. This was never performed,
and was only published in 1964, with an introduction by Michael
Timko indicating that Wells for a time had serious thoughts of
becoming a dramatist. In *Hoopdriver's Holiday*, he turned a cautious, lightweight comedy into something approaching a social
problem play. Just before the final curtain Hoopdriver is left
alone on the stage, bitterly denouncing the middle-class family who
have just cold-shouldered him, and the social system in general:

> "It isn't fair! It isn't fair! I never 'ad a chance! I was
> shoved into that shop before I was fourteen. I got no
> education. . . . I got no ideas! Fourteen. . . . When 'er sort
> of chaps are going off to their Etons and their
> 'Arrows. And then they turn and scoff at you! What am
> I? I'm a thing to measure linen and pack parcels . . . a
> sort of white nigger! Me in Sydenham! . . . A country
> ought to be ashamed to turn out a man like me.
> I'm done for. I've woke up too late! What can I do now?"
> (*Moment of perfect meditation.*) "I'll do *something*. . . . If I
> kill myself to do it!" (*He turns about as if seeking for
> something to do.*)
>
> Curtain [17]

This is raw and crude as drama, but it shows Wells drawing in a
much wider range of feelings than in *The Wheels of Chance*.
Anger and social protest are the essential preliminaries to his
mature comedy.

In *Kipps* (1905) they are transmuted into the brilliant portrayal
of the hero's childhood and apprenticeship. At the beginning
Kipps is free, open and undefined. His parents have died in un-
specified circumstances, leaving only a few vague memories, and
he lives with an uncle and aunt who are remote, inanimate figures.
But he is the nucleus of a marvellously solid and tangible little
world:

He knew all the stones in the yard individually, the creeper
in the corner, the dustbin and the mossy wall, better
than many men know the faces of their wives. There was
a corner under the ironing-board which, by means of a
shawl, could be made, under propitious gods, a very
decent cubby-house, a corner that served him for several
years as the indisputable hub of the world, and the stringy
places in the carpet, the knots upon the dresser, and
the several corners of the rag hearthrug his uncle had
made, became essential parts of his mental foundations.[18]

These are the earliest data of his being. Both here and in "The
Door in the Wall", Wells's view of childhood may be compared
to Wordsworth's. The child is not altogether dissociated from
his environment; later, the prison-house shades descend. At first
Kipps's fluid individuality expresses itself in a rich variety of roles
—he plays at red Indians, warriors, shipwrecked sailors, and
smugglers. But soon a straitjacket of social conventions and
prohibitions is imposed upon him, until the broad sympathies of
his early imaginative life become atrophied and perverted. The
process begins with some painful lessons in table manners and
continues at school, but full-scale subjugation only begins when
he enters the drapery at Folkestone. *Kipps* contains Wells's fullest
and bitterest description of the apprentice's life. The conditions
are those which he himself knew, but they undergo a creative
transformation comparable to that which Dickens wrought on
the social institutions in his novels. Kipps's first tour of the
Emporium with the proprietor has a hallucinatory quality.[19]
Shalford prides himself on his "System", an attempt to regulate
his business as if it were a clockwork mechanism, by means of
petty rules, a strict hierarchy, and penny-pinching economies.
As each employee becomes aware of the boss's approach, he
snaps into his position in the "System", "exactly like an automaton that is suddenly set going", and Kipps's split-second vision
of them in the privacy of their own activities takes on the unreality
of an optical illusion. The theme of dehumanisation is pursued in
Carshot, forever murmuring "My Heart and Liver"; in Shalford's

notices which always end "By Order"; and in his mutilation of language into a system of commercial telegraphese. Kipps, who at first has "no more System than a bad potato",[20] is eventually worn down into submission. It is a cramped and limited life. There are certain measures of enjoyment and self-development— flirtations with the Emporium's young ladies, learning refinement and becoming a "Masher", and even attending woodwork classes. Individuality of a kind lives on in the spirited uncouthness which is the only remnant of his childhood imaginative state. But these things are circumscribed by our knowledge of his situation. Kipps has been broken into his place in society, and he is a fully-formed draper.

This is only part of the story, however, and indeed *Kipps* was originally conceived as a great comic panorama entitled *The Wealth of Mr Waddy*.[21] Only a third of the original material survives in the published form. It is the only one of Wells's novels to employ a conventional Victorian plot structure. Since the drapery is represented as a lifelong dead end, Kipps clearly has to escape somehow, and this is contrived through the discovery that he is the heir of a Mr Waddy. Suddenly he finds himself a man of means and leisure, the owner of a house on the sea front, and an eligible bachelor. He becomes an unnaturally good bourgeois, punctilious in his observation of the preposterous genteel conventions and eagerly exchanging his freedom for the new bondage of afternoon calls, dinner parties and smart hotels. Wells, in fact, takes his hero on a comic journey through the English class system. A rebellion against the social traps that are laid for him becomes inevitable. It is prepared for by the revival of his childhood romance with the girl next door, Ann Pornick, and by his meeting with her brother and his friend Masterman— exponents of socialism whose function is to suggest the violence and greed beneath the mannered surface of genteel society. When Kipps does rebel, he plunges through the surface and returns to the homely simplicity of Ann. After further adventures, the tale of frustrations and humiliations is over, and he ends up happily as a country bookseller. *Kipps* is a sprawling, capacious novel in the Dickens mode, a mixture of comedy of manners, *Bildungsroman*, socialist tract, and modern folk-tale (the last element being virtually all that survived in the musical adaptation, *Half a Sixpence*). It is held together by Wells's most characteristic structural device, the cycle of suppression and release. Twice Kipps frees himself from claustrophobic social confinement, in acts of energetic and anarchic rebellion. He owes the first escape to his legacy, but this stroke of luck is a direct consequence of the wild, drunken night which leads to dismissal from the drapery. The second escape occurs when Kipps breaks out of a dinner party, and rushes down to the servants' quarters to propose to Ann, threatening to throw himself off the pier if she rejects him. These melodramatic acts are paralleled in Wells's story, "The Purple Pileus", where the henpecked shopkeeper, Mr Coombes, attempts to commit suicide by eating toadstools. But instead of poisoning him, they transform him into a raving fury of self-assertion. This is not a story of any great moral depth; Coombes's escapade simply makes him a more masterful husband. But the pattern is repeated with much greater intensity in *Mr Polly*, where the great Fishbourne fire burns out the traces of the hero's mental subjection. These stories of individual release are connected with "The Door in the Wall", discussed in the previous chapter; in each case Wells depicts an unforeseen rebellion against society and its appointed roles, a rebellion of the Freudian id against the ego and super-ego, with the character freeing himself through an act of self-destructive abandon. The pattern of individual release culminates in *Mr Polly*, where it leads to a deliverance from the deterministic world with revolutionary implications. "If the world does not please you, *you can change it*",[22] he discovers.

In making Kipps and Polly symbolic figures whose individual actions follow a representative pattern, Wells was departing considerably from the norm of realistic portrayal. His characters are evidently stylised; A. J. P. Taylor has described them disapprovingly as "caricatures or Humours" rather than real people,[23] implying that Wells was a bad case of the distortions inherent in the comic sense of life. In an interesting essay by John Holms (1928), Wells's sole literary achievement is found to be the begetting of an "authentic comic creation", the figure of the "little man".[24] Neither critic suggests the terms in which we could discriminate between different orders of caricature or comic creation; between Polly and the figures in a *Punch* cartoon, or his contemporary Billy Bunter. The condition which all these figures have in common is the detached and external viewpoint from which they are seen, so that they tend to become object-lessons. But detachment can lead to anything from a jeer to a poem or a system of sociology. In Wells at his best, there is a play of observation around his character which is both intellectually considered and imaginatively profound.

His method of characterisation expresses his scientific as well as his comic instincts. Henry James wrote to him that in *Kipps* he had "handled (the English lower-middle class) vulgarity in so scientific and historic a spirit", avoiding the picturesque and romantic "interference" of Dickens, Thackeray, and George Eliot.[25] This is a remarkable claim, which few would take at its face value. The late nineteenth century saw a widespread reaction against narrative "interference". Novelists after Flaubert sought to achieve an enhancement of realism through the discipline of artistic impersonality—the novelist as camera-eye rather than the novelist as puppet-master. No English-speaking novelist was more deeply interested in this movement than James himself. Wells, on the other hand, roundly attacked what he called the "'colourless' theory of fiction",[26] declaring that "The theory of a scientific, an impersonal standpoint, is fallacious".[27] He preferred the discursive, moralising commentary used by the Victorians, and this led him into frequent wrangles with Arnold Bennett, who accused him of artistic conservatism. His claim to be considered a "scientific" novelist, in fact, lies in the nature of his personal intrusions and not in their absence. James must have meant that he had given a closer and more objective explanation of his own class than had been achieved before; it is as if he were an anthropologist, or one of his own scientific explorers, bringing back news of the strange tribe whom James saw on his daily walks. The comedies abound in moments of pointed observation, picked out with Wells's unfailing eye for the typical; no modern novelist has caught the savour of English social consciousness more acutely. There

is Old Kipps, who falls in rapidly with the revised ambitions
caused by his nephew's private income: "Y'ought to 'ave a
bit o' shootin' somewheer".[28] And a snatch of dialogue which
shows how society helps its exploited shop-assistants to achieve
self-respect:

> Buggins resumed reading. He was very much excited
> by a leader on Indian affairs. "By Jove!" he said, "it
> won't do to give these here Blacks votes."
> "No fear," said Kipps.
> "They're different altogether," said Buggins. "They
> 'aven't the sound sense of Englishmen, and they 'aven't
> the character. There's a sort of tricky dishonesty about 'em
> —false witness and all that—of which an Englishman has
> no idea. Outside their courts of law—it's a pos'tive
> fact, Kipps—there's witnesses waitin' to be 'ired. Reg'lar
> trade. Touch their 'ats as you go in. Englishmen
> 'ave no idea, I tell you—not ord'nary Englishmen. It's in
> their blood. They're too timid to be honest. Too slavish.
> They aren't used to being free like we are, and if you gave
> 'em freedom they wouldn't make a proper use of it.
> Now, *we*—Oh, *Damn!*"
> For the gas had suddenly gone out, and Buggins had
> the whole column of Society Club Chat still to read.[29]

It is lights out in the Emporium: but as long as you can read the
Daily World Manager for an hour or so beforehand, you know that
you are free. This is a comedy based, not on individual eccentri-
cities, but on the supposition that men are unconsciously circumscribed and controlled by their social environment. Wells
takes a taxonomic view of character, arranging and classifying
it according to larger generalisations. His "scientific" aims,
which place him with Balzac and Zola rather than with
Flaubert and James, are summed up in a phrase from *Tono-
Bungay*—"social comparative anatomy". The opening sentences
of *Tono-Bungay* contain Wells's principal statement of the
taxonomic attitude. The speaker is George Ponderevo, the hero-
narrator:

Most people in this world seem to live "in character";
they have a beginning, a middle and an end, and the three
are congruous one with another and true to the rules of
their type. You can speak of them as being of this
sort of people or that. They are, as theatrical people
say, no more (and no less) than "character actors". They
have a class, they have a place, they know what is
becoming in them and what is due to them, and their
proper size of tombstone tells at last how properly they
have played the part. But there is also another kind of life
that is not so much living as a miscellaneous tasting of
life. One gets hit by some unusual transverse force, one is
jerked out of one's stratum and lives crosswise for the
rest of the time, and, as it were, in a succession of
samples. That has been my lot, and that is what has set me
at last writing something in the nature of a novel.

Wells's radical indifference to the conventional wisdom of the
novel is strongly evident here. The inherent dangers of an excessively schematic attitude to character were realised in most of his
later novels. But in the comedies and in *Tono-Bungay* he made the
"sociological novel" into a wholly imaginative form. Minor
characters like Buggins and Old Kipps are both living "in character", and the size of their tombstones may already be predicted.
Of young Kipps, too, Wells writes that after a time at the Emporium his sorrows "grew less actute, and, save for a miracle, the
brief tragedy of his life was over".[30] It takes a complex, scientific
intelligence to comprehend the limitations of ordinary people.
George Ponderevo's "miscellaneous tasting of life" has produced
this superior awareness. Wells had had the same opportunities,
and it is no accident that George is shown as a natural novelist.
Kipps and Polly are also hit by a "transverse force" and jerked
crosswise. They become conscious of their subservience, but after
the brief moment of rebellion and displacement they settle down
in a new "character" which is equally fixed and yet capacious
enough for them to fill in comfort. This individual transfiguration
solves no social problems. It is simply the discovery of an oasis of

undisturbed happiness within the desert of oppression. Kipps ends
up in a small shop, having lost most of his fortune; he would be in
financial trouble but for a lucky investment with a struggling
playwright. The shop is a sort of pastoral no-man's land between
the frontiers of leisured gentility and those of economic subjection.
The suggestion of pastoral is expanded in *Mr Polly*, where the grey
realities of the hero's early life give way to the Potwell Inn and a
lyrical vision of an England steeped in utopian primitivism.

Kipps ends with a receding and patronising effect which is too
distinctly Edwardian in tone to be very acceptable today. Almost
the last words are Kipps's recognition of his own uniqueness: "I
don't suppose there ever was a chap quite like me before".[31]
Richard Ellmann, who sees the hero's journey as a quest for self-
fulfilment, has written that "He is himself at last".[32] This would
be out of tune with the didactic ending of *Love and Mr Lewisham*,
and, in fact, we do not see Kipps achieving self-discovery. As
David Lodge says in a highly suggestive article, there is a "hollow
note"[33] to the comedy. Wells intrudes with a narrative aside ("I
am an old and trusted customer now"[34]), affirming the truth of
Kipps's story. The hero is now a carefully distanced small shopkeeper who still splutters out his words in heavily accentuated
cockney. We see him, in the words of the book's subtitle, as a
"Simple Soul". He has found a way of life and the sense of tranquillity, but there is and will always be a complex dimension of
living which eludes his awareness:

> Out of the darknesses beneath the shallow weedy stream
> of his being rose a question, a question that looked up
> dimly and never reached the surface. It was the question of
> the wonder of the beauty, the purposeless, inconsecutive
> beauty, that falls so strangely among the happenings
> and memories of life. It never reached the surface of
> his mind, it never took to itself substance or form; it
> looked up merely as the phantom of a face might look,
> out of deep waters, and sank again into nothingness.[35]

The rather too misty and picturesque image seems to be put in
for Kipps's benefit, and writer and reader are felt to be better

equipped to articulate the question than he is. But the passage also has the sense that before the fundamental questions of life we are all on the same level. An impression of parity between narrator and hero is essential for the success of this comic method, and it is much more securely achieved in *Mr Polly*. In the following passage the narrator is still a controlling presence, but the flow of sympathy is as strong as the sense of detachment:

> He came to country inns and sat for unmeasured hours talking of this and that to those sage carters who rest for ever in the taps of the country inns, while the big, sleek, brass-jingling horses wait patiently outside with their wagons. He got a job with some van people who were wandering about the country with swings and a steam roundabout, and remained with them three days, until one of their dogs took a violent dislike to him, and made his duties unpleasant. He talked to tramps and wayside labourers. He snoozed under hedges by day, and in outhouses and hayricks at night, and once, but only once, he slept in a casual ward. He felt as the etiolated grass and daisies must do when you move the garden roller away to a new place.[36]

Most of this is plain, apparently neutral narrative, with the slow prose-rhythms suggesting the somnolent and regular passage of time in this half-idyllic rural world. The right moment for the personal intrusion is carefully chosen; it harmonises perfectly with the preceding description, and yet firmly and authoritatively interprets Polly in his released state, adding to his imaginative dimensions: "He felt as the etiolated grass and daisies must do when you move the garden roller away to a new place." This is a fresh variation on the theme of naturalness, and also a microcosm of the interpretation of life and the scale of values which inform *Mr Polly* as a whole. The garden roller is society, and once it is off his back he can continue to grow untrammelled. At such a moment the character makes a jump into immediacy, focusing our attention on the act of imaginative invention itself. At its best, this narrative method does not set the characters free, but enacts a series of renewals of their original setting-forth in the author's mind. The result is an interplay between third person narrator and simple hero, which in turn produces an interplay of social and personal assumptions. Wells both sees his hero from above, and sees with him from below; he measures his limitations from outside, and presents his vitality from inside. In this transmutation of his attitude to his own earlier life as a draper's apprentice, there is a curious mixture of collectivism and individualism. The taxonomic narrative emphasises the hero's relative simplicity and typicality; but at the same time Wells makes solitary heroes out of people whom most novelists would relegate to a subordinate role. Dickens created many communities of minor lower-class characters, but there is no Dickens hero who does not establish his connexions with the gentry. Nor are Kipps and Polly redeemed by the intellectual gifts, the articulateness or the fine moral insight of so many modern protagonists. In playing the spotlight of the novel on the comedy and poignancy of essentially limited lives, Wells was doing something genuinely new.

5

TONO-BUNGAY AND MR POLLY:
THE INDIVIDUAL AND
SOCIAL CHANGE

Wells's powers as a social novelist are most fully realised in *Tono-Bungay* (1909) and *The History of Mr Polly* (1910). Formally the two novels are in open contrast. *Tono-Bungay* is a social panorama, a "description", as Edward Shanks put it in an admirable survey of Wells (1923),[1] "in a multitude of instances, of how human nature expressed itself in England in the twentieth century". It is cast as the autobiography of a complex, stubbornly intellectual engineer. *Mr Polly* is a poetic comedy built around the most memorable of Wells's simple heroes, and exhibiting some highly singular instances of human nature. In *Tono-Bungay*, the Ponderevos, uncle and nephew, are always moving forward on their social journey, and the narrative sweeps along with a mounting exhilaration. It ends aboard a destroyer racing out to sea. Mr Polly becomes a tramp wandering about the countryside, and he finally attains to a tranquil dignity, having moved through an emotional cycle which has the stately frequency of a human lifetime. The two novels of Wells's artistic maturity have several themes in common, but they offer a striking confirmation of V. S. Pritchett's remark that "Wells, as an artist, thrived on keeping his seeds of self-contradiction alive".[2]

In *Tono-Bungay* he was concerned, perhaps more directly than any other twentieth-century novelist, with the nature of social change. "An old and degenerating system, tried and strained by new inventions and new ideas";[3] Wells detected only shifting uncertainties behind the Edwardian façade of permanence, and

soon after *Kipps* appeared he began the elaborate planning of a
major novel diagnosing the social condition and exploring the
typical expressions of human value within it. In the opening
sections of *Tono-Bungay* George Ponderevo indicates the vast
areas of experience which seem to him relevant. The only limit
to his ebullience seems to be spiritual exhaustion:

> I suppose what I'm really trying to render is nothing more
> nor less than Life—as one man has found it. I want to
> tell—*myself*, and my impressions of the thing as a
> whole, to say things I have come to feel intensely of the
> laws, traditions, usages, and ideas we call society, and how
> we poor individuals get driven and lured and stranded
> among these windy, perplexing shoals and channels.[4]

After *The New Machiavelli*, James wrote to Wells remonstrating
about "the bad service you have done your cause by riding so
hard again that accurst autobiographic form which puts a premium
on the loose, the improvised, the cheap and the easy".[5] He had
evidently felt the same about *Tono-Bungay*. George warns that
the novel will be "something of an agglomeration", and adds
that his "ideas of a novel all through are comprehensive rather
than austere".[6] Recent critics have been divided as to whether the
novel Wells actually wrote with "restraint and care"[7] is the one
that George warns us to expect. Mark Schorer, Arnold Kettle,
and Walter Allen all find a lack of inner artistic unity; Kenneth B.
Newell and David Lodge, on the other hand, have discovered an
extraordinary amount of thematic integration, repetition, and
intensification, and my own reading supports their view.[8] If
Tono-Bungay was to present a panoramic vision of a changing
society, it needed a sound and extensive basis of social analysis.
David Lodge, who sees it as a "Condition of England novel" in
the tradition of Disraeli, Mrs Gaskell, and the Dickens of *Hard
Times*, gives a brilliant exposition of the taxonomic view of
society developed in the narrative. George's descriptive commentary both links the multitude of experiences and phenomena
which he encounters, and animates them with "a strange and
sinister life of their own".[9] It is a diseased life; Wells creates a

network of pathological images of growth, decay, hypertrophy, and malignancy, radiating from a central organic metaphor for the condition of England—cancer. One of the many passages expressing the idea of sinister and malignant growth is George's survey of the newly swollen London of his time. He concludes a splendid topographical evocation by relating the formless tracts of the suburbs to an organic conception of the city (the "affected carcass") as a whole:

> All these aspects have suggested to my mind at times, do suggest to this day, the unorganised, abundant substance of some tumorous growth-process, a process which indeed bursts all the outlines of the affected carcass and protrudes such masses as ignoble, comfortable Croydon, as tragic, impoverished West Ham. To this day I ask myself will those masses ever become structural, will they indeed shape into anything new whatever, or is that cancerous image their true and ultimate diagnosis? . . .[10]

The idea of social cancer has a considerable nineteenth-century history, from Cobbett (the "Great Wen") and Carlyle to Gissing, and it has re-emerged more recently in Norman Mailer's theories of the hipster. Wells had hinted at it in "The Days to Come", when Denton raved against civilisation as a "vast lunatic growth".[11] There are precedents, too, for the rhetorical technique of *Tono-Bungay* in Dickens, Zola, and in the images of the class system in *Kipps*. Wells's earlier novel is full of oppressive institutions: the Emporium, the Royal Grand Hotel at which Kipps stays in London, *Manners and Rules of Good Society* (his guide-book), Chester Coote his chaperon, and the Anagram Tea with its bewildering crowd of people wearing incomprehensible labels. These are drawn together in the titanic symbol of the Labyrinthodon at Crystal Palace, and the System is summed up at last, with a Dickensian staginess, in an even more generalised image of an obsolete monster:

> As I think of them lying unhappily there in the darkness, my vision pierces the night. See what I can see!

> Above them, brooding over them, I tell you there is a
> monster, a lumpish monster, like some great clumsy
> griffin thing, like the Crystal Palace labyrinthodon, like
> Coote, like the leaden goddess of the Dunciad, like some
> fat, proud flunkey, like pride, like indolence, like all
> that is darkening and heavy and obstructive in life. It is
> matter and darkness, it is the anti-soul, it is the ruling
> power of this land, Stupidity. My Kippses live in its
> shadow. . . . And the claw of this Beast rests upon them![12]

This is a drastic oversimplification; it is the whole system, and not
parts of it, that Kipps encounters at every stage, and Wells has
only to pin it down, encircle it and destroy it with rhetoric in
order to rescue his hero from the enchantment. Name the system
as Stupidity—a prehistoric monster which will perish of its own
accord—and it is already half-extinct. There is a more genuine
social insight in an incidental passage from the chapter entitled
"The Housing Problem". Kipps and Ann, looking for a house
to buy, are appalled by the avoidable domestic drudgery imposed
by basement kitchens, crude plumbing, and the narrow, dangerous
stairs up which coal and water have to be carried:

> All the houses they saw had a common quality for which
> she could find no word, but for which the proper word
> is "incivility". "They build these 'ouses," she said,
> "as though girls wasn't 'uman beings."[13]

Incivility; the word penetrates at once through the comedy of
polite manners in which Kipps has so earnestly engaged. His
experience gives a very complete account of the travesties of
"civility".

In *Tono-Bungay* the monster Stupidity is replaced by a historical
analysis of English society, which is superbly recapitulated in the
final scene, as the destroyer sweeps down the Thames cleaving a
section through all the strata of English history. The last hundred
years have seen the withering of the organic society represented
by Bladesover, the country house in which George spends his
boyhood, and the atrophy and hypertrophy brought by the spread

of commercialism and profiteering. The condition of England, as George surveys it, is compared to "an early day in a fine October".[14] The underlying rot and decay are thinly masked by the Edwardian Indian summer. The new forces of socialism, science, and technology point ahead to the winter and spring, but the society they will create remains an enigma. This alone leads to an outlook very different from that of *Kipps* and *Mr Polly*, where society is a constant pressure upon the individual. George moves in an area of flux—the sea across which his destroyer drives, or the air across which the rocket of Tono-Bungay, the patent medicine, flashes. He is one of the new men, and he owes his social opportunities to his uncle Edward Ponderevo, inventor of Tono-Bungay, the jumped-up "little man" who becomes a great financier, and whose rise and fall provides both the novel's broad shape and comic vitality, and George's most intimate and revealing insights into the rot in English society. George begins as an orphan, and is whirled up into the "pseudo-morphous" commercial aristocracy; for him, as for Wells himself, the world of confinement and submission is located back in his childhood. Under the Bladesover system, he recalls, "every human being had a 'place'"[15] in a graded hierarchy. Bladesover was an organic society because its members co-operated to support one another's sense of function and station. The point is made in the sly observation of Lady Osprey behaving "rather like an imitation of the more queenly moments of her own cook",[16] and it is forced home in one of Wells's greatest comic scenes, the servants' tea at Bladesover which is the epitome of genteel stuffiness. Wells's organic society makes a pointed contrast with that of D. H. Lawrence, who wrote approvingly in *The Rainbow* of the imaginative enrichment brought to the women of Cossethay by the lady of the Hall, whose "life was the epic that inspired their lives".[17] For Wells the relation is a dead one, and the mental images it provides are hung with cobwebs:

> "Sir Roderick used to say," said Mrs. Mackridge, "that the First Thing"—here Mrs. Mackridge paused and looked dreadfully at me—"and the Second Thing"—here

she fixed me again—"and the Third Thing"—now I was
released—"needed in a colonial governor is Tact." . . .
"It has always stuck me that that was a Singularly True
Remark."[18]

The country-house system has determined the shape of English
society as a whole, and anyone outside it is "perpetually seeking
after lost orientations". George is a natural child of Bladesover
and an instinctive rebel, but he never despairs of making his
escape, as Kipps and Polly do. He sees that the "old habitual
bonds"[19] have weakened, and the system is in open decline.

This slackening of social bonds leaves the way open for the
adventurer riding a "transverse force" of his own creation, and the
principal personal conflicts in *Tono-Bungay* do not begin until the
release has been achieved. The first stage in the Ponderevos'
emancipation is their discovery of the city. Edward, a chemist in a
typical country town of the Bladesover system, is forced to move
to London by impending bankruptcy. George follows him in
order to become a science student. At first he is deeply disillusioned.
His first move after leaving Bladesover took him to Chatham,
where he was appalled by the dingy squalor of industrialism.
He observed that the surplus of population from the landed
estates were herded into places which reminded him strongly in
colour and smell of the Bladesover dustbins;[20] industry "in a
landlord's land" lives off the scraps and sewage of the organic
society.

George continues to use Bladesover, the starting-point of his
experience, as a key to decipher each new environment, and his
"social anatomy" of London is a brilliant example of this. Central
London, with its parks, West End mansions and clubs, museums,
art-galleries and libraries, Bond Street, Harley Street and the City,
is the consummation of the country-house culture. But it is
surrounded by the vast, tumorous growths of the East End and
the suburbs, threaded by the railways which have even butted
their termini in among the mansions. The residential areas, the
"dingy London ocean",[21] remind George of Chatham, and the
description is crowded with images of waste and dirt. But as

George's knowledge of the metropolis becomes more intimate, and he ceases to be a priggish scholarship boy up from the provinces, his view changes. London is like a sea, a formless element of flux which erases fixed personal identities. He becomes socially "invisible" in an alluring, anarchic environment which will mould itself to his fantasies. The restless, ambivalent curiosity of adolescence is aroused by the hoardings, the people in the streets, the public meetings and freedom of thought, and the beckoning prostitutes: "Extraordinarily life unveiled".[22]

For George, the threat to his own identity is linked with sexual stimulation. Edward, who began playing the Stock Exchange to relieve the tedium of Wimblehurst, nourishes much grander dreams:

> "London, George," he said, "takes a lot of
> understanding. It's a great place. Immense. The
> richest town in the world, the biggest port, the greatest
> manufacturing town, the Imperial city—the centre of
> civilisation, the heart of the world! See those sandwich
> men down there! That third one's hat! Fair treat!
> You don't see poverty like that in Wimblehurst, George!
> And many of them high Oxford honour men, too.
> Brought down by drink! It's a wonderful place,
> George—a whirlpool, a maelstrom! whirls you up and
> whirls you down."[23]

This is a new world of infinite possibilities and inconceivable degradation, and Edward prepares to grab his chance. When Tono-Bungay whirls him up, he breaks into song with the words "I'm afloat, I'm afloat", and his financial ventures are known as "flotations". George too wishes to master the anarchic element, the sea, and he ends up building destroyers. The direct social analysis in *Tono-Bungay* shows England as a carcass swollen by cancer and hypertrophy. The narrative itself, following the journeys of Edward and George, contrasts two ways of living in the turbulent and disordered regions of the organism. Here I would go further than David Lodge, who finds the frame of social analysis to be "the only constant element in a novel which is otherwise deliberately chaotic in structure".[24] Wells's network of metaphors is not confined to George's commentary. It penetrates to the core of the protagonists themselves, so that George and Edward exist both as realised characters, and as the poetic embodiments of opposing and yet not wholly incompatible values.

Edward is first of all a comic character, seen with detachment and invariably through George's eyes. He owes little to conventional ideas of the tycoon, for he remains a small shopkeeper, a typical Wellsian figure (except for his energy) who is blown up big by a social accident. He is first seen jerking in and out of his shop in carpet slippers to inspect his eccentric window-display, a thwarted little man fighting external subjection with the obscure inner compulsions of his fantasy. There is a homely and ineffectual quality about him which contrasts at all times with the social havoc he causes; George, with his habitual taxonomy, characterises this as "Teddiness". The justly famous death-scene, which Wells modelled on his visit to his dying friend, George Gissing, enforces the point that for all the splendour of his ascent from a Clerkenwell back-street to the huge mansions of Lady Grove and Crest Hill, Edward's greatest projects, like Mr Polly's, are inherently spiritual. It is entirely fitting that he should leave the world babbling of cloud-capped towers and gorgeous palaces,[25] and after his death George confesses to feeling as the audience feels at the end of a play.[26] Each of Edward's appearances is a tableau. The narrative dwells at great length on the houses, the gestures, and the clothes which mark the different stages in his progress. The title of one of the earlier chapters—"The Dawn Comes, and my Uncle appears in a New Silk Hat"—is characteristic of the method, as are phrases such as "There he stands in my memory" and "So he poses for my picture". Edward, in fact, is revealed by a montage technique; he is an automaton, and all his projects and ideas are self-expressive, glimpses of an inner romance that by some freak fits in with the madness of the world. He is the focus of the sparkle and vitality in the novel, and yet his commercial activities provide the dramatic context for Wells's social criticism. There is always a limit to the narrative indulgence of his wilful, obsessive behaviour. The note of disapproval creeps in when he cheats George out of his mother's legacy, and his callous treatment of the admirable Aunt Susan (whose cheerful stoicism points to the deficiencies in both George and Edward) inevitably limits the reader's sympathy for him. Edward is called "Napoleonic" about twenty times in the novel, and although this accounts for some of his grandeur, Wells takes care to insinuate his own view of Napoleon as a monster of blind and petty egotism. *The Outline of History* (1920) is enlivened by a fierce attack on the man whom Wells now saw as the greatest of all traitors to the historical process. Humanity, in his view, was emerging slowly from a scatter of warring tribal groups towards global unity. In 1799 (much as in 1909), the old order was degenerate and dying, and "strange new forces drove through the world seeking form and direction".[27] But Napoleon, the man of the hour, was impervious to this unrivalled opportunity. Wells makes him an archetype of the purely expressive nature, the incarnation of libido: "What we all want to do secretly, more or less, he did in the daylight."[28] And what he did do was to "strut upon the crest of this great mountain of opportunity like a cockerel on a dung-hill".[29] Whatever we think of this as history, we cannot mistake the involuntary echoes of *Tono-Bungay*. Crest Hill was Edward's greatest mansion. The indictment against Edward appears in one of the best moments of the novel, a dialogue in which George's friend Ewart intuitively seizes upon the difference between nephew and uncle:

> "Your nephew, sir, is hard; he wants everything to go to a sort of predestinated end; he's a Calvinist of Commerce. Offer him a dustbin full of stuff; he calls it refuse—passes by on the other side. Now, *you*, sir—you'd make cinders respect themselves."
>
> My uncle regarded him dubiously for a moment. But there was a touch of appreciation in his eye.
>
> "Might make 'em into a sort of sanitary brick," he reflected over his cigar end.

"Or a friable biscuit. Why *not*? You might advertise:
'Why are Birds so Bright? Because they digest their food
perfectly! Why do they digest their food so perfectly?
Because they have a gizzard! Why hasn't man a
gizzard? Because he can buy Ponderevo's Ashpit
Triturating Friable Biscuit—Which is Better.'"[30]

The general bearing of this is made clear in an acute and prophetic
comment on modern advertising—"The old merchant used to
tote about commodities; the new one creates values." But Ewart's
assessment makes the "Romance of Commerce" no more than
the adornment of waste. This connects up with the other dirt
and waste images in the novel—with Chatham and the London
suburbs, with the patent medicine itself (Tono-Bungay is "slightly
injurious rubbish" and in his more philanthropic moments
George would like to throw the whole stock down the drain),
and with the "quap", a radioactive mineral which George tries
to steal from the African coast. "Quap", which is explicitly
compared to the degenerative processes in society, is cancerous
stuff found in "heaps of buff-hued rubbish".[31] Edward's exploitation of rubbish is his exploitation of the whole society. Brilliant
like the cockerel, he is an emanation from the dunghill, a specimen
of human waste. This is a severe judgment on the comic hedonist,
who after all is indispensable to the novel. Soon afterwards Wells
was making handsome amends for his own and George's "Cal-
vinism", by writing *Mr Polly*.

Towards the end of *Tono-Bungay* George uses the idea of waste
to sum up not only his uncle but the content of his book and the
condition of England itself:

> I have called it *Tono-Bungay*, but I had far better have
> called it *Waste*. I have told of childless Marion, of my
> childless aunt, of Beatrice wasted and wasteful and
> futile. . . . It is all one spectacle of forces running to
> waste, of people who use and do not replace, the story
> of a country hectic with a wasting aimless fever of
> trade and money-making and pleasure-seeking. And
> now I build destroyers![32]

The final exclamation here is consciously ironical, and it is followed by another of George's momentary self-criticisms: "It may be I see decay all about me because I am, in a sense, decay." These admissions may put us on our guard, but since they call attention to the difficulties of any kind of interpretative sociology they do not have any precise effect on the way in which George is seen. The portrayal of George is the source of considerable flaws in the second half of the novel. Edward and George are plainly antithetical; the one is the sensualist embroidering life with his fantasies, the other the straightforward scientist who calls waste waste. It is George who confidently judges the people and the society around him, and who finally writes them off. His perceptions, also, provide the note of uplift which concludes the novel, as the destroyer steaming out to sea becomes a symbol of Technology driving forward through the waste. Few readers have found this affirmation—"Sometimes I call this reality Science, sometimes I call it Truth"[33]—entirely satisfactory. But it needs to be stressed that the "other note" George is now sounding, which he goes on to describe as "the heart of life" and "the one enduring thing", has been heard many times before. It is in fact the principle of George's character—the principle of drive.

Both the Ponderevos are socially displaced persons. George cannot live on his inner resources as Edward does, and he constantly searches for sources of nourishment outside himself. After the failure of his marriage he defines his temperament as a "stupid, drivingly-energetic, sensuous, intellectual sprawl".[34] This is intended as deprecating, and indeed, it describes a spiritual disorder no less than his uncle's, but George really feels that the driving energy redeems him. It *is* him, and it must be in his terms a state of grace. Yet his energy, both in his science and in his love affairs, leads him into a succession of failures. The process begins with his expulsion from Bladesover. Cut loose from life "in character". he discovers a "queer feeling of brigandage", and a compulsion to drive himself back into a station in society.[35] This initial insecurity is connected with a quality of bluntness, an impatience with pretence and concealment which informs all his attitudes. This leads to such telling social observations as his description of the

suffocating respectability of the Ramboat home with its drapes
and hangings. Marion Ramboat, George's girl-friend, is prin-
cipally responsible for this, since it is she who has "draped the
mirror, got the second-hand piano, and broken her parents
in."[36] Yet he is irresistibly drawn to her. Her exterior qualities
count for nothing against his urge for the "drawing back of a
curtain" to reveal "the reality of love beneath".[37] He cannot help
creating value where there is none; he marries her, and the only
reality he finds is disappointment. There are vividly realised
moments in the relationship, but it ends in formless meditations
and self-indulgent confessions. From now on George's self-
analysis becomes increasingly unsatisfactory, and the final claim
that he has come to see himself "from the outside—without
illusions"[38] is transparently false. He turns from the pursuit of
sexual fulfilment to the scientific quest for truth; the value of this,
it seems at one point, lies in the elusiveness of the goal, so that he
need never suffer disappointment:

> All my life has been at bottom, *seeking*, disbelieving
> always, dissatisfied always with the thing seen and the
> thing believed, seeking something in toil, in force, in
> danger . . . something I have ever failed to find.[39]

Science has been, he says, "something of an irresponsive mistress".
There is another irresponsive mistress in the book, however—
Beatrice Normandy, George's aristocratic playmate at Bladesover,
who returns into his life after his divorce—and his relationship
with her merely confirms the sense of displacement and loss of
identity. Most of the episodes are embarrassingly sentimental and
unreal, but the general intention is clear; love too has been displaced from the social hierarchy, and can only exist as moments of
totally unconnected privacy, a disentanglement from the world
which they recognise as spiritually akin to annihilation. The failure
of George's sexual relationships is symptomatic; he has been
knocked out of his place in society, he has lived "crosswise" and
seen through society, but he never makes a settlement and finds
a role as Kipps and Polly do. Whenever he aims at a fixed point,
it proves to be a chimera. Finally his drive is transferred to the

destroyer, rushing on heedlessly abreast of the chaos, "on what trail even I who made her cannot tell".[40] The only faith he has is in the activity of motion itself:

> I fell into thought that was nearly formless, into doubts
> and dreams that have no words, and it seemed good to me
> to drive ahead and on and on through the windy starlight,
> over the long black waves.[41]

Captain or passenger, driving or drifting, he is going nowhere, except out into the open future. The conclusion of *Love and Mr Lewisham* here receives a far more dramatic and paradoxical expression. "Science, power and knowledge are summed up at last in a destroyer", Mark Schorer has commented.[42] "As far as one can tell Wells intends no irony, although he may here have come upon the essence of the major irony in modern history." It can hardly be claimed, although those who see Wells as a naïvely optimistic rationalist might wish to do so, that he had no intimations of this particular irony. He knew that you have to destroy in order to rebuild, and in all his imaginative prophecies it is through catastrophe that men are brought to their senses. The destroyer symbolises the paradoxes inherent in the two main twentieth-century ideologies of progress—revolutionary theory and scientific humanism. To attempt to control the environment is to risk defeat, and to have reached a scientific analysis of people and society, as George's life shows, is to have cut oneself off from their sources of nourishment. The question remains to what extent *Tono-Bungay* embodies the ironies it raises. All the elements of failure and uncertainty are there in the novel, but they are subdued beside the exhilaration of the sense of change itself. A comparison may be made here with a novel on a similar theme, Scott Fitzgerald's *The Great Gatsby*. I will take the closing sentence from each:

> So we beat on, boats against the current, borne back
> ceaselessly into the past. (Fitzgerald.)
>
> We are all things that make and pass, striving upon a
> hidden mission, out to the open sea. (Wells.)

The last note of *Tono-Bungay* is an ambiguous one. The "hidden mission" leaves it open whether the striving is enough to overcome the current, whether it signifies control or submission. Fitzgerald, on the other hand, uses the same image for an elegant statement of futility. His studied detachment, which clearly belongs to the novel as art, is vulnerable to the reply which Wells's narrator made to the Time Traveller: "If that is so, it remains for us to live as though it were not so."[43] *Tono-Bungay* offers a devastating picture of commercialism and social stagnation, and Wells clearly felt the need for a final profession of faith. As a result, he both endorsed George's way of "living as though it were not so" and acknowledged some of the objections to it; the weakness, the lack of conviction which prevents *Tono-Bungay* from achieving greatness, is that he could not find a better way. George, like Edward and of course like Wells himself, has something Napoleonic about him. "We make and pass," he writes; and he, too, fights against insignificance with a drivingly-energetic assertion of personality. *Tono-Bungay* remains a rich and exhilarating novel as long as it has two contrasted heroes; at the end, when Edward has left for his heavenly mansions, it is overwhelmed by a single, garrulous performance.

The History of Mr Polly is a small-scale novel beside *Tono-Bungay*, but in it Wells brought his lower-middle class hero close to perfection. Polly is a richer character than Kipps, and he lives out an inner romance like Edward. But his imagination supplies him with pastoral images and with queerly expressive idioms rather than with slogans and products, and he meets with far more resistance from the world than his predecessor. His is an ordinary life of frustration and defeat which culminates in a magnificent rebellion. But although he fights a lone battle for spiritual independence, his triumph is not purely an individual one. Wells broadens the significance of the comedy, using the interpretative narrative to show him as a socially representative figure. One of his devices is a carefully distanced exponent character, the "Highbury gentleman", who generalises about the "ill-adjusted units" produced by a "rapidly complicating society" defective in its "collective intelligence". Modern society, for him, is analogous to

a man who takes no thought of dietary or regimen, who
abstains from baths and exercise and gives his appetites
free play. It accumulates useless and aimless lives,
as a man accumulates fat and morbid products in his
blood; it declines in its collective efficiency and vigour,
and secretes discomfort and misery. Every phase of its
evolution is accompanied by a maximum of avoidable
distress and inconvenience and human waste. . . .[44]

Here Wells is repeating the diagnosis and the imagery of *Tono-
Bungay. Mr Polly* concentrates on the condition of the individual
rather than the condition of England, but this simply means that
the organic-social analogy is reversed. The metaphor of social
cancer is replaced by the metaphor of Polly's indigestion. The
novel begins with a picture of the hero in early middle age. He is
sitting on a gate, racked with dyspepsia and cursing the world
in his own idiom: "*Beastly* Silly Wheeze of a hole!" The relation
of dyspepsia and the world's beastliness, of inner and outer disorder, is explored in a passage two pages later:

> To the moralist I know he might have served as a figure
> of sinful discontent, but that is because it is the habit of
> moralists to ignore material circumstances—if,
> indeed, one may speak of a recent meal as a circumstance—
> seeing that Mr. Polly was circum. . . . So on nearly every
> day in his life Mr. Polly fell into a violent rage and
> hatred against the outer world in the afternoon, and never
> suspected that it was this inner world to which I am
> with such masterly delicacy alluding, that was thus
> reflecting its sinister disorder upon the things without. It is
> a pity that some human beings are not more transparent.
> If Mr. Polly, for example, had been transparent, or
> even passably translucent, then perhaps he might
> have realised, from the Laocoon struggle he would have
> glimpsed, that indeed he was not so much a human being
> as a civil war.
> Wonderful things must have been going on inside
> Mr. Polly. Oh! wonderful things. It must have been

like a badly managed industrial city during a period of
depression; agitators, acts of violence, strikes, the
forces of law and order doing their best, rushings to and
fro, upheavals, the *Marseillaise*, tumbrils, the rumble and
the thunder of the tumbrils. . . .[45]

Thousands of Pollys make up a diseased society; Polly himself is
torn by internal strife. The intestinal "civil war" which controls
his jaundiced view of the world is itself a consequence of social
disorder—it was provoked by unwise feeding in childhood and
his wife's appalling cookery—and it is turning him into a revolutionary, so that the strikes, tumbrils, and so on function as images
of his coming insurrection. The interchangeability of inner and
outer realities is neatly indicated by the play on "circum". The
stomach and the world, in fact, reflect one another like mirrors.
There is a thread of "indigestion" references throughout the book,
and connected with these is another pervasive analogy, that of
body and mind. Polly is torn by mental and physical conflict; both
derive from the ravages of his youth, when "His liver and his
gastric juice, his wonder and imagination"[46] were constantly at
war with the formative and educational processes of society. A
richly ironic association is suggested between the imagination and
the equally useless appendix. Polly's education is grotesquely seen
as an incredibly hamhanded surgical operation. The "surgeons"
—a "well-meaning, boldly enterprising, but rather overworked
and underpaid butcher boy" and a "left-handed clerk of high
principles but intemperate habits" (that is to say, a National school
and a private school) are fortunately unsuccessful. The "appendix"
is left "like a creature which has been beaten about the head and
left for dead but still lives".[47] The wound heals up, so that he
retains an obscure awareness of what Yeats called "the loveliness/
That has long faded from the world"; and in time his drab outward career coexists with a furtive but richly eventful fantasy life.
Once again, his imagination is seeking a capacious enough range
of roles to fill. Wells expresses his aspirations through a series of
lists—his boyhood fantasies, his favourite books, his meticulous
preparations for his suicide attempt, and finally his multifarious

duties as odd-job man at the Potwell Inn. Then there are the
impotent daydreams which flow continuously through his adult
life, manifesting a decorous sexuality and a romantic medievalism
which are familiar escapist elements in the Victorian and Edwardian
sensibility. The keynote of his imaginative individualism, however,
is the active reorganisation of his world through his garbled,
private language. "Allittritions Artful Aid"; "lill dog"; "Teles-
sated pavements all right" (an obscure reflexion of his panic as he
walks up the aisle to be married); "Boil it some more, O'Man":
Polly's expressions become more astringent as his life increases in
bitterness, and each of them is a momentary victory in his conflict
with the world. He transforms the oppressive reality into the
richer image of his fantasies, as Edward Ponderevo turns dung into
advertising jingles. But Polly's gift also leads to disaster. He uses
his linguistic gifts to fascinate his female cousins, their response
goes to his head, and he finds himself trapped with fifteen years of
dreary wedlock before him. Once Polly has escaped from his wife
and his shop, we hear little more of his linguistic inventiveness.
Having changed his world objectively, he no longer needs it.

For most of his life, Polly is the victim in a deterministic world.
Wells portrayed the forces of society and nature in many remarkable shapes, and none more so than those of Mr and Mrs Johnson,
Aunt Larkins, Uncle Pentstemon and the other characters brought
together in the magnificent funeral and wedding scenes of *Mr
Polly*. The extent to which Wells's comedy is indebted to Dickens
has often been noted. Wells even tried to persuade his publisher
to continue *Mr Polly* in an indefinite number of periodical parts,
and as a free wanderer, having thrown off the yoke of society,
Polly might have become a sort of Pickwickian tramp. This was
not to be, but one of the things which Wells clearly learnt from
Dickens, and adapted to his own purpose, was the symbolic power
of scenes of marred festivity. Dickens shows his humbugs and
scoundrels making a travesty of celebration, as in little Paul's
christening in *Dombey & Son*: "The party seemed to get colder
and colder, and to be gradually resolving itself into a congealed
and solid state, like the collation round which it was assembled."[48]
Wells shows how celebration itself, through its archaic rules and

conventions, can travesty the emotional spontaneity of the individual. Polly is an outsider at his father's funeral and his own
wedding. The superb description of him viewing his father's body,
for example, captures the embarrassing gulf between the free,
uncertain consciousness and the rigid traditional conventions of
feeling:

> His cousin Johnson received him with much solemnity,
> and ushered him upstairs to look at a stiff, straight,
> shrouded form with a face unwontedly quiet, and, it
> seemed, by reason of its pinched nostrils, scornful.
> "Looks peaceful," said Mr. Polly, disregarding the scorn
> to the best of his ability.
> "It was a merciful relief," said Mr. Johnson.
> There was a pause.
> "Second—second Departed I've ever seen—not counting
> mummies," said Mr. Polly, feeling it necessary to say
> something.
> "We did all we could."
> "No doubt of it, O'Man," said Mr. Polly.
> A second long pause followed, and then, to Mr. Polly's
> great relief, Johnson moved towards the door.[49]

There follow the ceremonial meals, and the noisy collisions of
fixed personalities incapable of communication but united by
kinship, the conventions and a common greed. There are similarities with the jealousy and suspicion of Polly's neighbours in
Fishbourne High Street. In each case, the bickering is an external
manifestation of the war in Polly's stomach.

Polly tries unobtrusively to escape from the funeral and wedding, but each time he is foiled. More desperate expedients are
suggested by a vivid memory of his father, struggling to get a sofa
up a narrow flight of stairs:

> For a time his father had coaxed, and then groaned like a
> soul in torment, and given way to blind fury; had sworn,
> kicked, and struck at the offending piece of furniture,
> and finally, with an immense effort, wrenched it upstairs,

with considerable incidental damage to lath and
plaster and one of the casters. That moment when self-
control was altogether torn aside, the shocked discovery
of his father's perfect humanity, had left a singular
impression on Mr. Polly's queer mind. . . .

    A weakly wilful being, struggling to get obdurate things
round impossible corners—in that symbol Mr. Polly could
recognise himself and all the trouble of humanity.[50]

His father becomes a general symbol of man in an alien universe,
and this prepares for the broad, allegorical reference of his own
release. When it comes, his self-control is torn aside in an instinctive act of assertion linked with the death-wish. The affair of the
Fishbourne fire has a grandiosity appropriate to Polly's fantasies.
Ironically, however, his instincts save him, and the shock of fear
which turns his suicide attempt into panic and flight brings about a
spiritual resurrection. The fire is described with energy and demonic
gusto, and David Lodge has rightly called it a "private enactment
of the earlier visions of global destruction"[51] in the scientific
romances. The result of this deluge, however, is liberation, as the
deterministic world collapses around him. He "understood there
was no inevitable any more, and escaped his former despair".[52]

He finally settles down in the idyllic Potwell Inn, in an idyllic
and sexless relationship with the woman who owns it. It is here
that he fulfils his fantasies, notably in the violence of his mock-
heroic backyard scrap with the petty criminal Uncle Jim. This is
a consummation of his romantic medievalism in knight-errantry,
in defence of a riverside inn which itself has a strong literary and
pastoral flavour. *Mr Polly* ends, in fact, as a Thames valley
romance, a late example of a favourite Victorian genre which
includes Arnold's "Thyrsis" and "The Scholar-Gipsy", Morris's
News From Nowhere, some of the verses in the *Alice* books, and
Jerome K. Jerome and Kenneth Grahame. Wells was also drawing
upon his own memories of a Thames-side inn, Surly Hall near
Windsor, where he spent some holidays as a boy. And the
tranquillity in which Polly comes to rest has a regressive element
which is not only literary:

It was one of those evenings serenely luminous, amply and
atmospherically still, when the river bend was at its
best. A swan floated against the dark green masses of the
further bank, the stream flowed broad and shining to
its destiny, with scarce a ripple—except where the reeds
came out from the headland, and the three poplars rose
clear and harmonious against the sky of green and yellow.
It was as if everything lay securely within a great,
warm, friendly globe of crystal sky. It was as safe and
enclosed and fearless as a child that has still to be born. It
was an evening full of the quality of tranquil,
unqualified assurance. Mr. Polly's mind was filled with the
persuasion that indeed all things whatsoever must needs
be satisfying and complete. It was incredible that life
had ever done more than seemed to jar, that there could
be any shadow in life save such velvet softnesses as made
the setting for that silent swan, or any murmur but the
ripple of the water as it swirled round the chained
and gently swaying punt.[53]

It is certainly remarkable that *Kipps*, *Tono-Bungay*, and *Mr Polly*
all conclude with these watery scenes. But the symbolic womb into
which the landscape, the sky and the whole universe now dissolve
is the distinguishing feature of the passage quoted. It points to a
complexity of resolved and unresolved meaning, for it ought to
be understood in Wells's terms as well as Freud's. If we do so, it
becomes the keystone of the arch of organic-social analogies in
the book, and curiously analogous to the destroyer in *Tono-
Bungay*. The destroyer suggests a dialectic of creation and destruction which has its counterpart in Wells's political projects for the
future. After the fire, Polly has sloughed off the corrupted skin of
training and servility which was all society had to offer him. He
is back where he started; an "artless child of Nature, far more
untrained, undisciplined, and spontaneous, than the ordinary
savage",[54] who is released into a world accommodated to his
nakedness. Wells, I think, might have justified the mellow conclusion to *Mr Polly* by seeing the "friendly globe of crystal sky"

as the womb in which the new civilisation and the new human race could be born. This would make Polly a forebear, and his fulfilment as well as his victimisation would have a general significance. But the argument cannot be pressed too far. The friendly sky embraces a literary landscape steeped in nostalgia; the womb metaphor is cosy and soothing, with none of the bracing development of embryonic life. Life, in fact, is drawing to a close, and after an orgy of satisfying primitivism Polly has achieved the "smooth, still quiet of the mind".[55] The moral questions raised by Wells's comic hedonist are not clearly resolved. Polly is so obviously right in his anarchistic struggle for a richness of which he has been cheated except in dreams; Edward Ponderevo is equally wrong in choosing the path marked out by his obsessions. The dedicated scientist or revolutionary, however austere his imagination, is also driven to impose his will on society. It is not the wilfulness but the social acceptability of the capitalist adventurer which is so damning. There is a telling moment in the Wimblehurst section of *Tono-Bungay* when George describes his uncle's dreams of cornering quinine. George imagined then that anyone attempting this would be sent to prison; later experience teaches him that anyone who actually brought it off would be much likelier to end up in the House of Lords.[56] It is unlikely that Wells himself was ever in any real danger of being offered a peerage, and he continued to play the *enfant terrible,* coming out with a vehement attack on the monarchy only a few months before his death. But David Lodge very plausibly suggests that, although he condemned the British social system as "essentially irresponsible", he "secretly . . . felt his own success had been contingent on that irresponsibility";[57] hence his ambiguous attitude to his irresponsible comic heroes. There is nothing Napoleonic about Mr Polly, and the indulgence of his libido could never lead him to profit by the system, so the comedy of his limited life ends in a fitting and deeply-felt individual triumph. But this ending is still not as closely linked to Wells's broad "world outlook" as he had wished the boat at Sandgate to be. The good life, he wrote in *First and Last Things*, is that which "contributes most effectively to the collective growth".[58] Polly's solution is attained on the simple and pastoral level, and it only doubtfully possesses the qualities which Wells as a moralist required on the intellectual and complex. If David Lodge is right in postulating a secret guilt about his own success, the question must be why Wells was unable to bring what could hardly have been a unique phenomenon out into the open; why, in fact, his analysis of George Ponderevo is deficient. Wells was more conscious of his intellectual assumptions than most novelists, and perhaps the weakest part of the "reconstruction of the frame" of the universe which he inherited in the eighties and nineties was its account of individual psychology. His characterisation shows him anticipating some of the main insights of modern psychoanalysis, but he was not able to develop them as fully as he might have done had he formed his imagination after Freud as well as after Darwin. After 1910 he began to lose interest in imaginative character-creation. He would still write a few social comedies—*Bealby* (1915) and *You Can't Be Too Careful* (1941) are examples —but these are of little significance. His later novels, as will be seen, preserve the seeds of sociological and ethical self-contradiction, but they are neither tended so carefully nor allowed to grow so luxuriantly.

6

THE DISCUSSION NOVELS

With the exception of *Ann Veronica* and *The New Machiavelli*, few of Wells's later novels have survived their initial welcome. Edward Shanks predicted that future generations would pay about as much attention to them as to Voltaire's tragedies;[1] Virginia Woolf concluded a review of *Joan and Peter* (1918) with the tart assurance that "the roar of genuine applause which salutes every new work of his more than makes up, we are sure, for the dubious silence, and possibly the unconcealed boredom, of posterity".[2] Recently, however, the publication of the Wells–James correspondence (in Edel and Ray's *Henry James and H. G. Wells*, 1958) has been followed by a revival of interest in Wells's artistic decline itself. His cruel debunking of James in *Boon*, and the magisterial rebuke from James which ended their fifteen years of friendship, are among the more spectacular episodes of modern literary history. James made what many have regarded as his maturest and most concise statement of artistic credo—"It is art that *makes* life, makes interest, makes importance. . . ."[3] Wells professed not to understand him, and ended his side of the affair with a gesture of renunciation—"I had rather be called a journalist than an artist".[4] Later he often pretended that this was what he had felt all along, stating with ringing untruth that he had "never taken any very great pains about writing",[5] and that he had seen the novel as "about as much an art form as a market place or a boulevard".[6] Unfortunately several of his critics, including such a reliable guide as Norman Nicholson in his *H. G. Wells* (1950), have been misled by this. Recent research by Professor Ray[7] has brought to light Wells's early book reviews, with their trenchant

concern for imaginative standards, and this alone should en-
courage us to look more closely at the stages by which he pro-
gressed from the artistry of *Tono-Bungay* in 1909 to his avowal of
journalism in 1915.

"We'll have a Republic in twelve years",[8] he had written to
R. A. Gregory in 1901. As the twelve years drew to a close, peers,
Ulstermen, suffragettes, and trade unionists found themselves in
open conflict with English society, and Wells himself grew more
outspoken in his rebellion. He quarrelled with the Fabian Society
in 1908, and so lost one outlet for his propaganda (*New Worlds for
Old*, a product of his Fabian period, is an eloquent statement of
orthodox Labour Party socialism). With Shaw, he had become
known as a spokesman for the enlightened intelligentsia, and in
1909 he published *Ann Veronica*, the story of a middle-class girl
who leaves her family to search for independence and sexual
fulfilment. It met with an outraged reception which is almost
inexplicable today. Another emancipated girl similar to Ann
Veronica appeared in *The New Machiavelli*, serialised in 1910;
the rumour spread that they were based on one of Wells's
mistresses, and the result was a clumsy smear campaign which re-
bounded on its organisers and brought him unprecedented popularity. "So far from extinguishing me," he wrote, "I have been given
an artificial and exaggerated importance. I have become a symbol
against the authoritative, the dull, the presumptuously established,
against all that is hateful and hostile to youth and tomorrow."[9]
The confident, fighting mood in which he was able to ride out this
scandal is reflected in the literary manifesto which marks this
phase in his work—"The Contemporary Novel", an address given
to the Times Book Club in 1911. This begins with a defence of the
spacious and discursive novels of Sterne and Dickens against the
formal rigour recommended by James and Conrad. He goes on
to repeat his old preference for a personal tone in the narrative,
and adds that the novelist must aim at more than realism of
description, since his art has "inseparable moral consequences".
It is, in fact, a "study and judgement of conduct".[10] In a stable
society, the novelist could simply reflect the established standards,
but in periods of questioning and moral uncertainty, any artistic

account of the social conflict is inevitably partisan. The novel must then be made a positive force for the growth of consciousness and social change; it must "appeal to the young and the hopeful and the curious, against the established, the dignified, and defensive":

> You see now the scope of the claim I am making for the novel; it is to be the social mediator, the vehicle of understanding, the instrument of self-examination, the parade of morals and the exchange of manners, the factory of customs, the criticism of laws and institutions and of social dogmas and ideas. It is to be the home confessional, the initiator of knowledge, the seed of fruitful self-questioning. Let me be very clear here. I do not mean for a moment that the novelist is going to set up as a teacher, as a sort of priest with a pen, who will make men and women believe and do this and that. The novel is not a new sort of pulpit; humanity is passing out of the phase when men *sit under* preachers and dogmatic influences. But the novelist is going to be the most potent of artists, because he is going to present conduct, devise beautiful conduct, discuss conduct, analyse conduct, suggest conduct, illuminate it through and through.[11]

This is one of many modern demands for an art which is politically and socially "committed". But it is also a response to a moment which has receded into history, the moment of achieving universal literacy. Wells's epithets for the novel suggest a whole range of social spheres and personal activities which writers are going to link up in instant contact. The novel, in fact, is to become the dominant mass medium of the age, a communications network shaping and consolidating the culture it serves. It is to perform many of the functions which broadcasting, television, and journalism have actually come to fulfil. This is a vision of the novel as a humane and civilising force, but it is notably indifferent to the idea of art. Imaginative fiction is not a distinct and separate species, and its only acknowledged values are those of general social intercourse.

In the books which followed this manifesto, Wells deliberately

D

began to dilute his fictional skills. As a young reviewer he had
invariably come down hard on the novelist who failed to bring his
characters to life. Two of his most scathing attacks were directed at
Grant Allen, a progressive novelist of ideas who was in many ways
a forerunner of the post-1911 Wells. He had dismissed Allen's *The
Woman who Did* (1895) both as a novel and as an ethical discussion.
"The problem of marriage concerns terrestrial human beings", he
wrote sarcastically; it couldn't be solved by a story about "the
offspring of a plaster-cast".[12] His review of *The British Barbarians*,
also in 1895, is even more outspoken in its youthful dogmatism:

> the philosopher who masquerades as a novelist, violating
> the conditions of art that his gospel may win notoriety,
> discredits both himself and his message, and the result is
> neither philosophy nor fiction.[13]

In a mellower vein, he reflected on "the distinctive inhumanities
of what one might call the 'exponent character', the superior
commentary", in his essay on George Gissing.[14] Meeting such
a character in a novel was like "getting into an omnibus and
discovering a respectably dressed figure of wax among the
passengers". But Wells, of course, never managed to do without
exponent characters. In the comedies he created a series of lively,
peripheral eccentrics whose ideological viewpoints are balanced
against the pragmatic, common-sense feelings of the heroes. In
Tono-Bungay the exponent character and the active hero were
united for the first time. But later he came to see carefully drawn
characters as an expendable luxury, exposition and argumentation
being his primary concerns. His object was to "get on to a discussion of relationships", dividing the characters into the actively
exponent and the passively exposed:

> In all (the discussion) novels the interest centres not upon
> individual character, but upon the struggles of common
> and rational motives and frank inquiry against social
> conditions and stereotyped ideas. The actors in them are
> types, therefore, rather than acutely individualised persons.[15]

On the one hand, in a novel like *Ann Veronica* Wells was broadening the subject-matter of fiction (hence the scandal), and he had hopes of broadening its human importance as well. "Before we have done," he announced in "The Contemporary Novel", "we will have all life within the scope of the novel".[16] On the other hand, he was increasingly becoming a "philosopher masquerading as a novelist". The conflict can be seen in *A Modern Utopia* (1905), which is prefaced by a "Note to the Reader", in which Wells discusses his formal problems. His aim is at once to portray an ideal state, to set out the philosophical and sociological assumptions behind it, and to show two contemporary persons discovering and reacting to the way of life within it. He had already achieved something of this narrative complexity in *The First Men in the Moon*: but *A Modern Utopia* was intended as a serious contribution to political thought. Wells recalls his difficulties in finding the appropriate form. The discursive essay, the dialogue novel, a form of "interplay between monologue and commentator", and the adventure narrative were all tried and rejected before the final shape—"a sort of shot-silk texture between philosophical discussion on the one hand and imaginative narrative on the other"— was arrived at. He compares the effect to that of a lecturer interspersing his talk with film of his travels. The whole project, of course, is misconceived; he is trying to cram too much in. The portrayal of the two terrestrial visitors is palpably crude, and the book has so little of the quality of the earlier romances that it might have been better to dispense with "imaginative narrative" altogether.

Ann Veronica (1909) is close to the mode of Wells's comedies, and it combines "philosophy" and "narrative" on more equal terms. The first few chapters introduce the world of an intelligent middle-class girl, rebelling against the stuffiness of a London suburb. It is a solid, recognisable world which we enter again in *Marriage* and in the odd scene in *The New Machiavelli*, and yet it is shallower, flatter, and less intimately seen than the world of Kipps and Polly. The second paragraph of *Ann Veronica* establishes the tone exactly:

She had a compartment to herself in the train from
London to Morningside Park, and she sat with both her

feet on the seat in an attitude that would certainly
have distressed her mother to see and horrified her
grandmother beyond measure; she sat with her knees up
to her chin and her hands clasped before them, and she
was so lost in thought that she discovered with a
start, from a lettered lamp, that she was at Morningside
Park, and thought she was moving out of the station,
whereas she was only moving in. "Lord!" she said.
She jumped up at once, caught up a leather clutch
containing note-books, a fat text-book, and a chocolate-
and-yellow-covered pamphlet, and leaped neatly from the
carriage, only to discover that the train was slowing down
and that she had to traverse the full length of the platform
past it again as the result of her precipitation. "Sold
again," she remarked. "Idiot!" She raged inwardly, while
she walked along with that air of self-contained serenity
that is proper to a young lady of nearly two-and-twenty
under the eye of the world.[17]

Her four words of jerky, downright self-expression stand out
charged with a living energy. This is the same comic method as
in *Mr Polly*; the character is led through a succession of jumps
into immediacy, each jump being followed by a relapse. The
moment of vitality often points a moral criticism of the world.
When Ann Veronica is handed a note from her father forbidding
her to go to a dance, we are told that "she had at first a wild,
fantastic idea that it contained a tip".[18] In contrast to *Tono-Bungay*
and *Mr Polly*, however, there is no thread of grotesque language
and striking metaphor connecting such moments together. Ann
Veronica's healthy spontaneity is a more conventional quality,
like hockey-sticks in the drawing-room; it lacks the note of
obsession. In the passage quoted it is surrounded by the clusters of
details, generalisations and contrivance which are the prose
counterparts of the stuffy bourgeois world. But these sentences
have another purpose; they make direct lateral references to
external society, with its views on the posture and behaviour
proper to a young lady. The individual experience is contained in

an immediate framework of explanation. The events are almost
entirely seen through Ann Veronica's own consciousness. It is
part of her rebellion that she should set out to be a rational young
woman, but Wells makes her thought-processes remorselessly
rational. Through her conceptualising he establishes his own
generalisations about the position of women or the generation
gap. She comes to see her father, for example, less as a person than
as a case:

> He stood, a little anxious and fussy, bothered by the
> responsibility of her, entirely careless of what her life was
> or was likely to be, ignoring her thoughts and feelings,
> ignorant of every fact of importance in her life, explaining
> everything he could not understand in her as nonsense and
> perversity, concerned only with a terror of bothers and
> undesirable situations. "We don't want things to happen!"
> Never had he shown his daughter so clearly that the
> womenkind he was persuaded he had to protect and control
> could please him in one way, and in one way only,
> and that was by doing nothing except the punctual
> domestic duties and being nothing except restful
> appearances. . . . He had no use for Ann Veronica; he had
> never had a use for her since she had been too old to
> sit upon his knee. . . . These realisations rushed into
> Ann Veronica's mind and hardened her heart against him.[19]

The whole situation is oversimplified, and the structure of a
tyrannical father's attitudes is pointed out in the interests of Wells's
taxonomy. Ann Veronica's more intimate emotions cannot be
reached in this way. Sometimes Wells seems to be nervously
replacing a glass case between himself and his specimen. Here she
is warding off an attempted rape:

> For some seconds she stood watching him, and both
> were thinking very quickly. Her state of mind would have
> seemed altogether discreditable to her grandmother.
> She ought to have been disposed to faint and scream at all
> these happenings; . . .[20]

In addition to Ann Veronica's moments of comic vitality, the novel comes alive in some well-observed documentary scenes, from suburban evenings to the suffragettes storming West-minster. The heroine goes through a series of incidents marking stages in her discarding of bourgeois illusions. She breaks through the "wrappered world" of the respectable middle class, whose mental subterfuges and suppressions are symbolised by their chintzes, drapes, and calico. (Wells also made this point in *Tono-Bungay*, and no doubt his feelings about it stemmed from his years behind the counter.) Most of the characters in *Ann Veronica* have something to hide. The heroine sees through them all, penetrating through the layers of reality until she reaches the core of life's meaning in her marriage to a biologist. The hidden reality, as in *Love and Mr Lewisham*, is itself biological—the onward struggle of the species—and Ann Veronica's unladylike exultation at the basic truths of love, mating and child-bearing makes her "as primordial as chipped flint".[21] The book ends in an atmosphere of embarrassing mutual uplift—Wells's world outlook simplified for immediate consumption. In its less didactic moments, however, *Ann Veronica* remains enjoyably fresh and observant.

The same can hardly be said of *The New Machiavelli* (1911), an ambitious novel in which Wells set out to survey the Edwardian political scene. *The New Machiavelli* is broad enough in conception to remind us of an earlier political novel of ideas, Disraeli's *Coningsby*: but it raises high expectations only to disappoint them. The title suggests a manual of modern statesmanship comparable to *The Prince*. Wells was fond of referring back to previous literary models in his later books: there are also *Boon*, deriving from Mallock's *The New Republic*; *The Undying Fire*, from the Book of Job; and *The Anatomy of Frustration*, from Burton's *Anatomy of Melancholy*. Richard Remington, Wells's first-person narrator, claims affinities with Machiavelli because his political career has ended in exile, and because he too has been torn between the "white passion" of constructive statesmanship and the "red passion" of sensuality.[22] He is, in fact, the scientist and the sen-sualist of the earlier novels rolled into one; a microcosmic theatre of the universal struggle of order against prevailing disorder, and a more isolated figure even than George Ponderevo. *The New Machiavelli* suffers at every stage of a comparison with *Tono-Bungay*, with its two heroes. "Muddle", "confusion", "planning", "construction" are the key words of Remington's social commentary, but these are terms of political jargon rather than subtle and suggestive instruments of social analysis. As a child Remington lives among the landscapes and cities he can construct from wooden bricks—the appropriate game for a future statesman— and he looks back on the haphazard suburbanisation of his native Bromstead (Bromley) during the same years. Bromstead stands later on in the book for the general experience of muddle, but compared to Bladesover it is a very impoverished reference-point, lacking in topographical clarity, in historical insight and above all in close integration with the narrator's experience. It might have appeared in almost any of the later novels, and part of the description is a re-working of an earlier piece of journalism. Bladesover, by contrast, belongs only to *Tono-Bungay*.

The best things in *The New Machiavelli* are the intermittently lively observation of the political scene, Remington's disillusion with the hollowness of established radicalism and the patchwork nature of the Liberal Party coalition, and the caricatures of the Labour Party leaders and Sidney and Beatrice Webb. Remington takes his constructive ambitions into the Tory Party, where he founds a political weekly expounding Wells's brand of élitism. There has been some anxious critical discussion of this move to the Tories,[23] but it might have been imprudent for Wells to portray an adulterous Labour or Liberal politician. The second half of the novel is marred by a strain of garish crudity, both in the descriptions of Remington's emotional states and in the political ideas which express his positive values. The first-person narration turns the dramatic irony of his self-defeat to little advantage, and the book's overall shape reflects his inner disharmony all too faithfully.

Marriage, undeservedly perhaps, is a forgotten novel beside the preceding two. Published in 1912, its broad subject is the need for a modern religion. Wells sets out to explore the question which Lawrence posed a few years later in *Women in Love*: "wherein does life centre, for you?"[24] It begins with a virtual parody of the *Ann Veronica* situation, with Marjorie Pope rebelling against her family and her family's choice of a suitor. The Popes are spending their summer holidays in a country vicarage, which allows Wells to emphasise their spiritual rootlessness; and beneath a surface realism he caricatures various forms of fashionable triviality. Their aspirations towards social and moral purpose, for example, are represented by the charitable movement of Aunt Plessington and Uncle Hubert. The guiding principle of the movement is to be "aggressively beneficial" towards the lower classes: but then, since "no people in England will ever admit they belong to the lower strata of society, Aunt Plessington's Movement attracted adherents from every class in the community".[25] The Plessingtons themselves are a caricature of the Baileys in *The New Machiavelli*, who in turn represented the Webbs. There is a similar air of stylisation about the other characters. Once these stilted people have been put through their paces, Wells allows his heroine, Marjorie, to escape. A high-minded research scientist—Richard Trafford, Wells's most idealised self-projection—arrives out of the sky in an aeroplane crash on the vicarage lawn, and the two rapidly fall in love and get married. The bland humour of the early scenes is dismissed; the seriousness with which Trafford and Marjorie build their lives shows them as potential members of a governing élite such as the "Samurai" of *A Modern Utopia*. But in spite of themselves the Traffords slip back into the social banalities they had thought to escape. Marjorie is emancipated but without a function, and she is drawn into the petty rivalries and extravagances of fashionable society. Trafford abandons pure research to become an industrial developer. This gradual entanglement, and their baffled awareness of it, are shown in great detail and with considerable subtlety; the effect is rather like that of one of George Gissing's middle-class novels, *The Whirlpool* (1897). But the later developments are seen increasingly within Trafford's consciousness, so that the novel becomes a report on the discoveries and adventures of an eminently Wellsian mind. The Traffords finally go off to Labrador for a year, and their disentanglement and spiritual regeneration are accomplished, once again, through a return to the primordial knowledge of life as struggle. Here Wells's "evolutionary mysticism" emerges, and the book ends as a sort of dramatised lay sermon. *Marriage* is a dogged attempt to infuse a propaganda purpose into the form of the novel as he had practised it. Great volumes of reagents with varying imaginative qualities are thrown into the vat, but the result is a half-brewed novel, in which a genuine portrayal of a relationship is only one element in the all-purpose Wellsian mixture.

The later novels are roughly of two kinds. In the first, Wells's mental dissociation of "philosophical discussion" and "imaginative narrative" is quite plain. The two strains are artificially yoked together in various ways, and the result is a collection of hybrids as odd as Dr Moreau's Beast Men. Wells shrugged off *The Passionate Friends* (1913) in a letter to James as "mixed pickles and I know it";[26] in fact he had written a conventional romantic novel as a vehicle for discussion material, and much the same is true of *The Wife of Sir Isaac Harman* (1914). *The Research Magnificent* (1915) could be seen as a sensationalised version of *Marriage* with the structural oddities of *A Modern Utopia*. *Joan and Peter* (1918) is a panoramic novel covering the previous thirty years of English history and mainly taken up by an exhaustive analysis of the educational system. Wells artlessly remarks in his *Autobiography* that this became too big to handle, and "The missing public-school stage is to be found in *The Story of a Great Schoolmaster*"[27]—the last-named book being his biography of F. W. Sanderson, the progressive Headmaster of Oundle. During the 1920s Wells's output of fiction slowed down somewhat. *Meanwhile* (1927) includes a vivid documentary picture of the General Strike, and here and in *The Autocracy of Mr Parham* (1930), he began to write anti-fascist propaganda. *Men Like Gods* (1923), though weak as fiction, is essential for the study of his utopian beliefs. A few more genuine novels emerged from his later years, although none of them can stand beside his major works. *Christina Alberta's Father* (1925) is the comic fable of a little man who comes to believe he is Sargon I, King of Kings; *Mr Blettsworthy on Rampole Island* (1928) and *The Croquet Player* (1936) are darker fables of human bestiality. One realistic novel from the last phase stands out: *Apropos o,*

Dolores (1938), an intimate, bitter comedy in which Wells gives a last twist to his contrast of scientist and sensualist types, and then diffuses it all in ponderous masculine self-justifications.

Mr Britling Sees It Through (1916) and *The World of William Clissold* (1926) are novels of a different kind. Like *The New Machiavelli* and *Marriage*, they move close to fictionalised autobiography, so that discussion and experience are not artificially yoked together, but united in the same sense as they were for Wells himself. Each of these novels contains an extended transcription of the garrulous mental activities of a single hero, a Wellsian self-projection who propounds analyses and formulations echoing those of Wells's non-fiction works. These novels are no better than those of the first kind, but they point more directly to the critical problems of Wells's later work.

Wells is a sociological novelist who relates the individual lives he presents to general patterns and classifications. In the comedies it is the narrator who points out the taxonomic aspect of the characters, and they are seen with detachment, as protégés, butts, or victims. In the discussion novels there is a tendency to create representative characters, achieving and articulating a comprehensive vision of life. Theirs may be the only voices heard. Remington, Britling, and Clissold inhabit a deterministic world where men are still subordinate to nature, but they are able to transcend it in their understanding of it, and not through acts of rebellion and release. The hero as victim gives way to the hero as prophet or social scientist. Once again he is an explorer, an explorer not of alien societies but of his own territory and his own mind. Trafford is one of these explorers, and a passage from *Marriage* will illustrate the mode of social observation in the discussion novels. He is visiting the East End:

> And about this sordid-looking wilderness went a
> population that seemed at first as sordid. It was in no sense
> a tragic population. But it saw little of the sun, felt the
> wind but rarely, and so had a white, dull skin that looked
> degenerate and ominous to a West-end eye. It was not
> naked or barefooted, but it wore cheap clothes that were

tawdry when new, and speedily became faded, discoloured, dusty, and draggled. It was slovenly and almost wilfully ugly in its speech and gestures. And the food it ate was rough and coarse if abundant, the eggs it consumed "tasted"—everything "tasted"; its milk, its beer, its bread was degraded by base adulterations, its meat was hacked red stuff that hung in the dusty air until it was sold; east of the city Trafford could find no place where by his standards he could get a tolerable meal tolerably served. The entertainment of this eastern London was jingle, its religion clap-trap, its reading feeble and sensational rubbish without kindliness or breadth. And if this great industrial multitude was neither tortured nor driven nor cruelly treated—as the slaves and common people of other days have been—yet it was universally anxious, perpetually anxious about urgent small necessities and petty dissatisfying things. . . .[28]

The emphasis here is upon the empirically verifiable. There is a generic description of appearances—the colour of the skin, the look of the clothes, the taste of the food—backed up by an appeal to common historical conceptions ("the slaves and common people of other days"). This "mass observation" approach is tempered with gestures towards shared experience. The passage hinges on the detail about the eggs; they "tasted", and the reticent inverted commas make a bold appeal to some association of unpleasant taste in the reader—"we all know what a stale egg is like; there is no more to be said". The appeal is ambiguous, however; would the "stale egg" experience be the same for the East Enders themselves? This ostensibly objective description gives us the reactions of a class of supposedly neutral observers, identifiable with Wells's readers, rather than the scene itself. Trafford stands for Wells, his readers, and the "West-end eye" which can judge because it knows the comfortable alternatives to tawdry clothes, anaemic skin, and adulterated food. The particularity of his point of view is stated only to be forgotten by the end of the paragraph, when his impatience with working-class entertainment and his apprehension of universal anxiety are presented as conclusive judgements on the society.

The class of neutral observers, or social scientists, is what Wells is out to create; it is the object of his propaganda. He liked to speak of himself as a "common man", and he did so in a curious double sense. At their meeting in 1934 Stalin was able to tell him succinctly and, one would think, conclusively, that "Important public men like yourself are not common men".[29] But in *Experiment in Autobiography* Wells wrote that everyone as he grew from family associations and childhood to the desirable condition of adult world citizenship, would become the "conscious Common Man of his time and culture".[30] In other words, as he acquired a fully-developed outlook on life, he would come to see himself as a unit member of a larger co-operative whole, the human species. Trafford, not Mr Polly, is the Common Man in this sense, for he is working towards a comprehensive awareness of human life. He is a forerunner of the world community Wells envisaged in which men would live harmoniously because their guiding ideas were commonly held. The ideal Common Man would presumably be someone who had solved the sociologist's dilemma of involvement and detachment, and had an exact and scientific knowledge of the human world to which he belonged.

Here we find both the motive and the difficulty of the novels Wells wrote expounding one man's "reconstruction of the frame" of the universe. In *The New Machiavelli* Remington writes that his purpose is "to show a contemporary man in relation to the state and social usage, and the social organism in relation to that man".[31] This is a possible attitude for an author to take to his character, and it is not unlike Wells's attitude in *Tono-Bungay*. But George himself is less schematic in his aims: "I want to tell—*myself*, and my impressions of the thing as a whole". Remington is undertaking to give a taxonomic view of himself, an objective analysis of his own social consciousness. When Wells or anyone else does this as a thinker, we are free to refute what he says. When a character in a Wells novel does it, there is the added implication that "this is normative vision". Without looking ridiculous the reader cannot answer back a Remington or a Clissold, as he could have engaged in polemic with Wells himself. The fictional convention enabled Wells to present his views and attitudes with a more hypnotic effect than in ordinary discursive argument, for if we believe in the character and the voice, we have gone a long way to accepting what he says. But the hypnotic power of these novels was inevitably short-lived. The Common Man in capitals is an idealist vision, an act of Wellsian faith, and once this is lacking, his appraisal of the world and himself comes to seem a tawdrily individual one. *The New Machiavelli* and the novels which follow it are set in a self-contained ruling-class circle which is established by the reintroduction of minor characters in book after book. The world, as in the East End passage, is always seen from the vantage-point which Wells attained as a successful writer. But although Trafford, Remington, and Clissold are all members of his intellectual élite, there is little sense of their collective existence as a class. Their main experience is solitary. At one stage Trafford muses upon kingship, imagining himself as a "sleepless King Emperor agonising for humanity".[32] Such a godlike, universal vision—the Whitmanesque assertion that "I am large, I contain multitudes"—easily becomes solipsism; the meaning of individual lives is a function of the collective, species existence, so that individuals are fully realised only as figments of the imagination that can comprehend the collective. Solipsism can be seen entering the novel when, for example, Wells creates a foil for Trafford, a character called Dowd whom Trafford privately calls "Dowd the Disinherited". It is this schematised Dowd who impresses himself on the reader of *Marriage*; his meeting with Trafford is that of Conscious Common Man and Proletarian Man. Wells's longest and most grandiose novel, *The World of William Clissold*, spreads this mode of vision over three volumes and nearly nine hundred pages. Clissold's avowal of artistic purpose is psychologically more sophisticated than Remington's:

> I should say that a description of my world best expresses what I have in view; my world and my will.
> I want it to be a picture of everything as it is reflected in my brain.[33]

Wells's object is to contribute to the collective definition of *our* world through the rendering of a specimen modern consciousness. But Clissold and his other universal personae have a curious point of resemblance to his comic heroes. They, too, are driven to realise their fantasies, although to do so, they must create whole worlds and whole novels in their own image. Once again there is no clear division between responsibility and self-indulgence. Wells wrote for many admirable political and social purposes, but he also wrote to impose himself totally on his readers. "The ground of the drama is somehow most of all in the adventure for *you*—not to say *of* you—", Henry James told him.[34] This is the "singleness of mind" of which Orwell complained, and it is also the ground of his enormous popular influence, for, as Orwell acknowledged, he succeeded in imposing himself. "Thinking people who were born about the beginning of this century are in some sense Wells's own creation."

Wells's world outlook was constrained and made acceptable by his impressive commitment to the facts of scientific discovery and the faculty of rational analysis. His recourse to the irresponsible magic of the fictional persona was not altogether consistent with this. As the science was superseded and the flaws of the reasoning became exposed, the currency of the late novels naturally ceased. But there is another way of imposing yourself on your readers which is more lasting in its effects. Every artist expresses his own "adventure", but he must somehow use the constraints of his chosen form to make good the deficiencies of merely personal experience. Wells did so in the scientific romances, through the alternation of imaginative worlds, and in the comedies, through the interplay between interpreting narrator and created hero. In this universe of plasticity and surprise, of images and types, the modes of scientific investigation and human response are combined. Microscopy is paired with the sense of wonder, taxonomy with the sense of fun. It is in these joint exercises of the scientific and literary imagination that his creative energy continues to renew itself.

REFERENCES

CHAPTER 1

1. W. Warren Wagar, *H. G. Wells and the World State*, p. 6
2. G. Orwell, *Collected Essays*, II, p. 143.
3. *Op. cit.*, II, p. 145.
4. *Op. cit.*, II, p. 142.
5. *This Side of Paradise*, Penguin edn. 1963, p. 189.
6. Quoted in Grant Richards, *Memories of a Misspent Youth*, London 1932, pp. 327–8.
7. *T.B.*, 1, 3, vii.
8. *P.*, 7, vi.
9. "Disentanglement as a Theme in H. G. Wells's Fiction", *Papers of the Michigan Academy* XXXIX (1954) pp. 439 ff.
10. C. P. Snow, *Variety of Men*, London 1967, p. 51.
11 "Mr Wells Explains Himself", p. 3.
12. *E.A.*, II, pp. 501–2.
13. J. Conrad, *The Nigger of the Narcissus*, London 1955, p. 21.
14. *T.B.*, I, I, iii.
15. *E.A.*, I, p. 136.
16. *E.A.*, I, p. 138.
17. *M.U.*, Appendix.
18. Wagar, p. 78.
19. T. H. Huxley, *Evolution and Ethics*, 1894, p. 40.
20. *Fortnightly Review*, LX (1896), p. 594.
21. *M.U.*, I, i.
22. Hillegas, *The Future as Nightmare*, New York 1967, pp. 63, 70, 79.
23. *The Discovery of the Future*, 1913, p. 60.
24. *Contemporary Review*, LXXII (1897) p. 200.
25. *Saturday Review*, LXXXIII (1897) p. 250.
26. *'42 to '44*, p. 169.
27. *Op. cit.*, p. 171.
28. *M.U.*, Appendix.
29. *The World of H. G. Wells*, New York 1915, pp. 20 ff.
30. *E.A.*, II, p. 619.

CHAPTER 2

1. Bernard Bergonzi, *The Early H. G. Wells*, p. 24.
2. *Op. cit.*, p. 41.
3. J. Conrad, *Life and Letters*, London 1927, I, p. 259.
4. *E.g.* Kingsley Amis, *New Maps of Hell*, London 1961, Ch. I.
5. E. Shanks, *First Essays in Literature*, p. 158.
6. *C.S.S.*, pp. 76–7.
7. V. S. Pritchett, *The Living Novel*, p. 116.
8. *The Food of the Gods*, III, 5, iii.
9. A. L. Morton, *The English Utopia*, p. 186.
10. *C.S.S.*, p. 63.
11. *C.S.S.*, p. 25.
12. *C.S.S.*, pp. 90–1.
13. Robert P. Weeks, "Disentanglement as a Theme in H. G. Wells's Fiction", p. 440.
14. From *The Puritan*, I (1899) p. 219.
15. *I.M.*, 20.
16. *I.M.*, 21.
17. *I.M.,*, 28.
18. *Atlantic edn.*, II, p. ix.
19. Bergonzi, pp. 104–5.
20. *Moreau*, 14.
21. Anthony West, "H. G. Wells", *Encounter*, pp. 52 ff.
22. *Moreau*, 22.
23. *Moreau*, 22.
24. *E.A.*, II, p. 543.
25. Bergonzi, p. 127.
26. *W.W.*, II, 6.
27. *W.W.*, I, 15.
28. *W.W.*, II, 7.
29. *W.W.*, II, 2.
30. *C.S.S.*, p. 412.
31. *W.W.*, II, 2.
32. *F.M.M.*, 24.
33. *F.M.M.*, 25.
34. Bergonzi, pp. 162–4.
35. *Arnold Bennett & H. G. Wells*, p. 265.
36. *F.M.M.*, 24.
37. *F.M.M.*, 4.
38. See Bergonzi, pp. 45 ff.
39. *F.M.M.*, 8.

CHAPTER 3

1. *F.M.M.*, 8.
2. *W.W.*, I, I.
3. *An Englishman Looks at the World*, pp. 192 ff.
4. J. Conrad, *Life and Letters*, I, p. 310.
5. *W.W.*, II, 3.
6. *F.M.M.*, 17.
7. *F.M.M.*, 23.
8. Bergonzi, *The Early H. G. Wells*, pp. 84 ff.
9. *C.S.S.*, p. 150.
10. *The Sleeper Awakes and Men like Gods*, London (Odhams) n.d.,
    Preface.
11. *Atlantic edn.*, v, p. ix.
12. *In the Days of the Comet*, I, 4, i.
13. See Note 10.
14. Hillegas, *The Future as Nightmare*, pp. 40 ff.
15. Bergonzi, pp. 152 ff.
16. J. Kagarlitski, *The Life & Thought of H. G. Wells*, p. 81.
17. *The Road to Wigan Pier*, Penguin edn. 1962, p. 178.
18. *C.S.S.*, p. 719.
19. *C.S.S.*, p. 786.
20. *C.S.S.*, p. 790.
21. *W.A.*, I, ii.
22. *W.A.*, I, iv.
23. *W.A.*, I, i.
24. *W.A.*, Epilogue.

CHAPTER 4

1. I. Raknem, *H. G. Wells and his Critics*, p. 45.
2. *Arnold Bennett and H. G. Wells*, p. 45.
3. *Saturday Review*, LXXXII (1896) p. 526.
4. *Henry James and H. G. Wells*, p. 105.
5. *Atlantic edn.*, VII, p. ix.
6. *L.L.*, 30.
7. *L.L.*, I.
8. *A Man from the North*, 1898, p. 265.
9. *L.L.*, 32.
10. *L.L.*, 23.
11. *E.A.*, II, p. 468.
12. *L.L.*, 31.

13. G. N. Ray, "H. G. Wells Tries to be a Novelist," *in Edwardians &
     Late Victorians*, pp. 121, 127.

14. *W.V.*, 30.

15. *K.*, I, 2, iii.

16. *Saturday Review*, LXXIX (1895) p. 676.

17. *Hoopdriver's Holiday*, p. 77.

18. *K.*, I, I, i.

19. *K.*, I, 2, i.

20. *K.*, I, 2, iii.

21. See *Atlantic edn.*, VIII, p. ix.

22. *P.*, 9, i.

23. "The Man who tried to work Miracles", in *The Listener*, 21. vii.1966,
     p. 81.

24. "H. G. Wells" in *Scrutinies*, ed. E. Rickword, London 1928, p. 149.

25. *Henry James and H. G. Wells*, p. 105.

26. *Saturday Review*, LXXXI (1896) p. 405.

27. *Saturday Review*, LXXX (1895) p. 843.

28. *K.*, I, 6, vi.

29. *K.*, I, 6, ii.

30. *K.*, I, 2, iv.

31. *K.*, III, 3, viii.

32. "Two Faces of Edward", in *Edwardians and Late Victorians*, ed. R.
     Ellmann, New York 1960, p. 199.

33. D. Lodge, *The Novelist at the Crossroads*, p. 217.

34. *K.*, III, 3, vii.

35. *K.*, III, 3, viii.

36. *P.*, 9, ii.

CHAPTER 5

1. *First Essays in Literature*, p. 164.

2. "Wells Marches On", in *New Statesman*, 23.ix.1966, p. 433.

3. *Atlantic edn.*, XII, p. ix.

4. *T.B.*, I. I, ii.

5. *Henry James and H. G. Wells*, p. 128.

6. *T.B.*, I, I, i.

7. *Atlantic edn.*, XII, p. ix.

8. M. Schorer, "Technique as Discovery", in *Forms of Modern Fiction*, pp. 9
    ff; A. Kettle, *Introduction to the English Novel*, London 1962, II, pp.
    92 ff.; W. Allen, *The English Novel*, London 1954, pp. 300 ff.; K.
    B. Newell, "The Structure of H. G. Wells's *Tono-Bungay*", in

English Fiction in Transition, pp. I ff.; D. Lodge, *Language of Fiction,*
pp. 214 ff.
9. Lodge, p. 219.
10. *T.B.,* II, I, i.
11. *C.S.S.,* p. 786.
12. *K.,* III, 2, V.
13. *K.,* III, I, ii.
14. *T.B.,* I, I, iii.
15. *T.B.,* I, I, iii.
16. *T.B.,* III, 3, iii.
17. *The Rainbow,* Penguin edn. 1949, p. II.
18. *T.B.,* I, I, iv.
19. *T.B.,* I, I, iii.
20. *T.B.,* I, 2, i.
21. *T.B.,* I, 3, vii.
22. *T.B.,* II, I, ii.
23. *T.B.,* I, 3, vi.
24. Lodge, p. 238.
25. *T.B.,* IV, I, vii.
26. *T.B.,* IV, I, viii.
27. *The Outline of History,* p. 620.
28. *Op. cit.,* p. 632.
29. *Op. cit.,* p. 620.
30. *T.B.,* II, 3, ii.
31. *T.B.,* III, 4, iv.
32. *T.B.,* IV, 3, i.
33. *T.B.,* IV, 3, iii.
34. *T.B.,* II, 4, ii.
35. *T.B.,* I, 2, iii.
36. *T.B.,* II, I, V.
37. *T.B.,* II, I, iv.
38. *T.B.,* IV, 3, iv.
39. *T.B.,* II, 4, x.
40. *T.B.,* IV, 3, ii.
41. *T.B.,* IV, 3, iii.
42. Schorer, *loc. cit.,* p. 17.
43. *C.S.S.,* p. 91.
44. *P.,* 7, iii.
45. *P.,* I, i.
46. *P.,* I, ii.
47. *P.,* I, ii.
48. *Dombey & Son,* London (Oxford U.P.) 1950, p. 60.
49. *P.,* 4, i.

50. *P.*, 4, i.
51. Lodge, *The Novelist at the Crossroads*, p. 217.
52. *P.*, 9, i.
53. *P.*. 10, iii.
54. *P.*, 10, i.
55. *P.*, 10, iii.
56. *T.B.*, I, 3, i.
57. Lodge, *loc. cit.*, p. 61.
58. *First & Last Things*, 1929, p. 79.

Chapter 6

1. E. Shanks, *First Essays in Literature*, p. 171.
2. Virginia Woolf, *Contemporary Writers*, London 1965, p. 93.
3. *Henry James and H. G. Wells*, p. 263.
4. *Op. cit.*, p. 264.
5. Introduction to Geoffrey West, *H. G. Wells*, 1930, p. 13.
6. *E.A.*, II, p. 489.
7. G. N. Ray, "H. G. Wells Tries to be a Novelist", pp. 106 ff.
8. W. H. G. Armytage, *Sir Richard Gregory*, London 1957, p. 46.
9. "My Lucky Moment", in *The View*, p. 212.
10. *An Englishman Looks at the World*, pp. 158–9.
11. *Op. cit.*, pp. 167–9.
12. *E.A.*, II, p. 550.
13. *Saturday Review*, LXXX (1895) p. 786.
14. *Contemporary Review*, LXXII (1897) p. 196.
15. *E.A.*, II, p. 477.
16. *E.A.*, II, p. 169.
17. *A.V.*, I, i.
18. *A.V.*, I, iv.
19. *A.V.*, 15, ii.
20. *A.V.*, 9, iv.
21. *A.V.*, 15, i.
22. *N.M.*, I, I, i.
23. See Geoffrey West, p. 168; I. Raknem, *H. G. Wells and his Critics*, pp. 106 ff.
24. *Women in Love*, Penguin edn., 1960, p. 63.
25. *Marriage*, I, 2, vii.
26. *Henry James and H. G. Wells*, p. 169.
27. *E.A.*, II, p. 500.
28. *Marriage*, III, I, i.

29. *New Statesmanship*, ed. Edward Hyams, London 1963, p. 107.
30. *E.A.*, II, p. 418.
31. *N.M.*, III, 4, i.
32. *Marriage*, III, 2, iv.
33. *The World of William Clissold*, I, I, ii.
34. *Henry James and H. G. Wells*, p. 167.

BIBLIOGRAPHY

I. H.G. WELLS

The best general bibliographies are *H.G. Wells: A Comprehensive Bibliography* by the H.G. Wells Society, 3rd edn., London 1972, and—for the earlier work—*The Works of H.G. Wells, 1887-1925: A Bibliography, Dictionary and Subject-Index* by Geoffrey H. Wells, London (Routledge) 1926. A remarkably comprehensive array of bibliographical information may be found in the *Catalogue of the H.G. Wells Collection in the Bromley Public Libraries*, ed. A.H. Watkins, London (Bromley Public Libraries) 1974.

1. *Collected Editions*

The Atlantic Edition of the Works of H.G. Wells, 28 vols. London (Unwin) and New York (Scribner's) 1924-7. An edition limited to 1,670 sets with approved texts and prefaces to each volume by H.G. Wells.

Seven Famous Novels by H.G. Wells. New York (Knopf) 1934, with the author's preface.

The Complete Short Stories of H.G. Wells. London (Benn) 1927.

The Favorite Short Stories of H.G. Wells. Garden City (Doubleday Doran) 1937.

2. *Fiction*

"The Chronic Argonauts", serial publication in *Science Schools Journal*, 1888. Reprinted in Barnard Bergonzi, *The Early H.G. Wells*, Toronto (Toronto U.P.) 1961, pp. 187 ff.

Select Conversations with an Uncle. New York (Merriam) 1895. Humorous essays and stories.

The Time Machine: An Invention. New York (Holt) 1895. Serial publication in *National Observer* and *New Review* 1894-5. For the serial versions, see *H.G. Wells: Early Writings in Science and Science Fiction*, ed. Robert M. Philmus and David Y. Hughes, Berkeley and Los Angeles (California U.P.) 1975, pp. 47 ff.

The Wonderful Visit. New York (Macmillan) 1895.

The Stolen Bacillus and Other Incidents. London (Methuen) 1895. Contains "The Stolen Bacillus", "The Flowering of the Strange Orchid", "In the Avu Observatory", "The Triumphs of a Taxidermist", "A Deal in Ostriches", "Through a Window", "The Temptation of Harringay", "The Flying Man", "The Diamond Maker", "Aepyornis Island", "The Remarkable Case of Davidson's Eyes", "The Lord of the Dynamos", "The Hammerpond Park Burglary", "A Moth—Genus Novo", "The Treasure in the Forest".

The Island of Dr. Moreau. New York (Stone & Kimball) 1896.

The Wheels of Chance: A Holiday Adventure. New York (Macmillan) 1896. *Hoopdriver's Holiday* (dramatised version written 1903-4), ed. Michael Timko. (*English Literature in Transition,* Purdue University, Ind.) 1964.

The Plattner Story, and Others. London (Methuen) 1897. Contains "The Plattner Story", "The Argonauts of the Air", "The Story of the Late Mr. Elvesham", "In the Abyss", "The Apple", "Under the Knife", "The Sea Raiders", "Pollock and the Porroh Man", "The Red Room", "The Cone", "The Purple Pileus", "The Jilting of Jane", "In the Modern Vein", "A Catastrophe", "The Lost Inheritance", "The Sad Story of a Dramatic Critic", "A Slip under the Microscope".

The Invisible Man: A Grotesque Romance. New York (Harper) 1897.

Certain Personal Matters. London (Lawrence & Bullen) 1897. Humorous essays.

Thirty Strange Stories. New York (Arnold) 1897. Includes "The Reconciliation", "The Rajah's Treasure", "Le Mari Terrible".

The War of the Worlds. New York (Harper) 1898.

When the Sleeper Wakes. New York (Harper) 1899. Revised as *The Sleeper Awakes,* 1910.

Tales of Space and Time. New York (Doubleday & McClure) 1899. Contains "The Crystal Egg", "The Star", "A Story of the Stone Age", "A Story of the Days to Come", "The Man Who Could Work Miracles".

Love and Mr. Lewisham. New York (Doran) 1899.

The First Men in the Moon. Indianapolis (Bowen-Merrill) 1901.

The Sea Lady: A Tissue of Moonshine. New York (Appleton) 1902.

Twelve Stories and a Dream. London (Macmillan) 1903. Contains "Filmer", "The Magic Shop", "The Valley of Spiders", "The Truth about Pyecraft", "Mr Skelmersdale in Fairyland", "The Story of the Inexperienced Ghost", "Jimmy Goggles the God", "The New Accelerator", "Mr. Ledbetter's Vacation", "The Stolen Body", "Mr. Brisher's Treasure", "Miss Winchelsea's Heart", "A Dream of Armageddon".

The Food of the Gods and How It Came to Earth. New York (Scribner's) 1904.

A Modern Utopia. New York (Scribner's) 1905.

Kipps: The Story of a Simple Soul. New York (Scribner's) 1905. A discarded early draft of this novel has been published as *The Wealth of Mr. Waddy,* Carbondale & Edwardsville (Southern Illinois U.P.) 1969.

In the Days of the Comet. New York (Century) 1906.

The War in the Air. New York (Macmillan) 1908.

Tono-Bungay. New York (Duffield) 1909.

Ann Veronica: A Modern Love Story. New York (Harper) 1909.

The History of Mr Polly. New York (Duffield) 1910.

The New Machiavelli. New York (Duffield) 1910.

The Country of the Blind, and Other Stories. London (Nelson) 1911. Includes "A Vision of Judgement" (1898), "The Country of the Blind" (1904), "The Empire of the Ants" (1905), "The Door in the Wall" (1906), "The Beautiful Suit" (1909).

The Door in the Wall, and Other Stories. New York (Mitchell Kennerley) 1911.

Marriage. New York (Duffield) 1912.

The Passionate Friends. New York (Harper) 1913.

The World Set Free: A Story of Mankind. New York (Dutton) 1914.

The Wife of Sir Isaac Harman. New York (Macmillan) 1914.

Boon. New York (Doran) 1915.

Bealby. New York (Macmillan) 1915.

The Research Magnificent. New York (Macmillan) 1915.

Mr Britling Sees It Through. New York (Macmillan) 1916.

The Soul of a Bishop. New York (Macmillan) 1917.

Joan and Peter. New York (Macmillan) 1918.

The Undying Fire. New York (Macmillan) 1919.

The Secret Places of the Heart. New York (Macmillan) 1922.

Men Like Gods. New York (Macmillan) 1923.

The Dream. New York (Macmillan) 1924.

Christina Alberta's Father. New York (Macmillan) 1925.

The World of William Clissold: A Novel at a New Angle, (2 vols). New York (Doran) 1926.

Meanwhile. New York (Doran) 1927.

Mr Blettsworthy on Rampole Island. New York (Doran) 1928.

The King Who Was a King. Garden City (Doubleday Doran) 1929.

The Adventures of Tommy. New York (Stokes) 1929. (Juvenile.)

The Autocracy of Mr Parham. New York (Doran) 1930.

The Bulpington of Blup. New York (Macmillan) 1933.

The Shape of Things to Come: The Ultimate Revolution. New York (Macmillan) 1933.

The Croquet Player: A Story. New York (Viking) 1937.

Star Begotten: A Biological Fantasia. New York (Viking) 1937.

Brynhild. New York (Scribner's) 1937.

The Camford Visitation. London (Methuen) 1937.

The Brothers: A Story. New York (Viking) 1938.

Apropos of Dolores. New York (Scribner's) 1938.

The Holy Terror. New York (Simon & Schuster) 1939.

Babes in the Darkling Wood. New York (Alliance) 1940.

All Aboard for Ararat. New York (Alliance) 1941.

You Can't be too Careful: A Sample of Life 1901-51. New York (Alliance) 1942.

3. *Political, Sociological and Philosophical Works*

Anticipations of the Reaction of Mechanical and Scientific Progress upon Human Life and Thought. London (Chapman & Hall) 1901.

The Discovery of the Future. London (Unwin) 1902. New York (B.W. Huebsch) 1913.

Mankind in the Making. London (Chapman & Hall) 1903. New York (Scribner's) 1904.

Socialism and the Family. London (Fifield) 1906.

New Worlds for Old. New York (Macmillan) 1908.

First & Last Things: A Confession of Faith and Rule of Life. New York (Putnam's) 1908. Revised edn. London (Watts) 1929.

"The Past and the Great State", in *Socialism and the Great State*, ed. H.G. Wells and two others. New York (Harper) 1912.

What Is Coming? A European Forecast. New York (Macmillan) 1916.

God the Invisible King. New York (Macmillan) 1917.

In the Fourth Year: Anticipations of a World Peace. New York (Macmillan) 1918.

The Idea of a League of Nations. Boston (Atlantic Monthly) 1919 (part-author).

History Is One. New York (Ginn) 1919.

Democracy under Revision. New York (Doran) 1927.

The Open Conspiracy: Blue Prints for a World Revolution. New York (Doubleday Doran) 1928.

The Common Sense of World Peace. London (Leonard & Virginia Woolf) 1929.

What Are We To Do With Our Lives? Garden City (Doubleday, Doran) 1931.

The Anatomy of Frustration: A Modern Synthesis. New York (Macmillan) 1936.

World Brain. New York (Doubleday, Doran) 1938.

The Fate of Homo Sapiens. London (Secker & Warburg) 1939. New York (Alliance) 1939, as *The Fate of Man.*

The New World Order. London (Secker & Warburg) 1939. New York
    (Knopf) 1940.

The Rights of Man. Harmondsworth (Penguin) 1940.

Guide to the New World. London (Gollancz) 1941.

The Outlook for Homo Sapiens. London (Secker & Warburg) 1942.

Science and the World-Mind. London (New Europe) 1942.

Phoenix: A Summary of the Inescapable Conditions of World Organisation.
    London (Secker & Warburg) 1942.

The Conquest of Time. London (Watts & Co.) 1942.

'42 to '44: A Contemporary Memoir. New York (Alliance) 1944. Includes
    Wells's "Thesis on the Quality of Illusion in the Continuity of
    Individual Life of the Higher Metazoa, with Particular Reference to
    the Species Homo Sapiens."

The Happy·Turning. London (Heinemann) 1945.

Mind at the End of Its Tether. London (Heinemann) 1945. With *The
    Happy Turning*, New York (Didier) 1946. The two volumes were
    reprinted as *The Last Books of H.G. Wells*, ed. G.P. Wells, London
    (H.G. Wells Society) 1968.

4. *Textbooks and Encyclopaedic Works*

A Textbook of Biology (2 vols.) London (W.B. Clive) 1893.

Honours Physiography (with R.A. Gregory). London (Joseph Hughes) 1893.

The Outline of History, Being a Plain History of Life and Mankind. New
    York (Macmillan) 1920. Revised edn. London (Cassell) 1972.

A Short History of the World. New York (Macmillan) 1922. Revised edn.
    London (Collins) 1965.

The Science of Life (3 vols) (with Julian Huxley and G.P. Wells). New
    York (Doubleday, Doran) 1931.

The Work, Wealth and Happiness of Mankind (2 vols). New York
    (Doubleday, Doran) 1931.

5. *Selected Journalism, etc*

Two recent anthologies of Wells's journalism are *H.G. Wells: Early
Writings in Science and Science Fiction,* ed. Robert M. Philmus and David
Y. Hughes, Berkeley and Los Angeles (California U.P.) 1975 (with
bibliography), and *H.G. Wells: Journalism and Prophecy 1893-1946,* ed. W.
Warren Wagar, Boston (Houghton Mifflin) 1965.

As yet there is no anthology of Wells's literary reviewing. For lists of his
unsigned fiction reviews, see Gordon N. Ray, "H.G. Wells Tries to be a
Novelist", in *Edwardians and Late Victorians,* ed. Richard Ellmann, New

York (Columbia U.P.) 1960, pp. 106 ff.; and "H.G. Wells's Contributions to the *Saturday Review*", in *The Library*, 5th ser. XVI (1961), pp. 29 ff. For details of his work as a dramatic critic, see Michael Timko, "H.G. Wells and 'the most unholy trade'", *English Language Notes* no. 1, June 1964, pp. 280 ff.

"The Woman Who Did", *Saturday Review* LXXIX (1895) pp. 319-20. Part reproduced in *Experiment in Autobiography*, pp. 549-51.

"Excelsior", *Saturday Review* LXXIX (1895) p.475. Reprinted in *Experiment in Autobiography*, pp. 411-13.

"Mr. Grant Allen's New Novel", *Saturday Review* LXXX (1895) pp. 785-6

"The Novel of Types", Saturday Review LXXXI (1896) pp. 23-4.

"Popular Writers and Press Critics", *Saturday Review* LXXXI (1896) pp. 145-6.

"The Lost Quest", *Saturday Review* LXXXIII (1897) pp. 249-50.

"The Novels of Mr. George Gissing", *Contemporary Review* LXXII (1897) pp. 192 ff.

"Stephen Crane from an English Standpoint", *North American Review*, August 1900, reprinted in *The Shock of Recognition*, ed. Edmund Wilson, New York (Doubleday, Doran) 1956, pp. 661 ff.

The Future in America: A Search after Realities. New York (Harper) 1906.

This Misery of Boots. London (Fabian Society) 1907. Boston (The Ball Pub. Co.) 1908.

"My Lucky Moment", in *The View*, 29. iv. 1911, p.212.

An Englishman Looks at the World. London (Cassell) 1914. New York (Harper) 1914 as *Social Forces in England and America.*

The War That Will End War. New York (Duffield) 1914.

The Elements of Reconstruction. London (Nisbet) 1916.

The War and the Future. London (Cassell) 1917. New York (Macmillan) 1917 as *Italy, France and Britain at War.*

Russia in the Shadows. London (Hodder & Stoughton) 1920. New York (Doran) 1921.

The Salvaging of Civilisation. New York (Macmillan) 1921.

Washington and the Hope of Peace. London (Collins) 1922. New York (Macmillan) 1922 as *Washington and the Riddle of Peace.*

A Year of Prophesying. London (Unwin) 1924. New York (Macmillan) 1925.

The Way the World is Going. London (Benn) 1928. Garden City (Doubleday, Doran) 1929.

After Democracy. London (Watts) 1932.

Stalin-Wells Talk. London (New Statesman & Nation) 1934. New York (New Century) 1947.

The New America: The New World. New York (Macmillan) 1935.
Travels of a Republican Radical in Search of Hot Water. Harmondsworth
(Penguin) 1939.
The Common Sense of War and Peace. Harmondsworth (Penguin) 1940.
Crux Ansata: An Indictment of the Roman Catholic Church. Harmondsworth
(Penguin) 1943. New York (Agora) 1944.

6. *Autobiography and Biography*

"Mr. Wells Explains Himself", *T.P.'s Magazine*, December 1911.
The Story of a Great Schoolmaster (F.W. Sanderson). New York (Mac-
millan) 1924.
The Book of Catherine Wells. Garden City (Doubleday, Doran) 1928.
Introduction by H.G. Wells.
*Experiment in Autobiography: Discoveries and Conclusions of a Very Ordinary
Brain—Since 1866*. New York (Macmillan) 1934.

7. *Letters*

Henry James and H.G. Wells, ed. Leon Edel and Gordon N. Ray. Urbana
(Illinois U.P.) 1958.
Arnold Bennett and H.G. Wells, ed. Harris Wilson. Urbana (Illinois U.P.)
1960.
George Gissing and H.G. Wells, ed. Leon Edel and Gordon N. Ray.
Urbana (Illinois U.P.) 1958.
Arnold Bennett and H.G. Wells, ed. Harris Wilson. Urbana (Illinois U.P.)
1960.
George Gissing and H.G. Wells, ed. Royal A. Gettmann, London (Hart-
Davis) 1961.

8. *Miscellaneous*

Floor Games. Boston (Small, Maynard) 1912.
Little Wars. Boston (Small, Maynard) 1913.
Things to Come. New York (Macmillan) 1935. Film Script.
The Man who could Work Miracles. New York (Macmillan) 1936. Film
script.

II. Others

For fuller lists see the H.G. Wells Society's *Comprehensive Bibliography*, (Books only); Geoffrey H. Wells's *Bibliography*, pp. 84 ff.; and the bibliography by Robert P. Weeks in *English Fiction in Transition*, 1 (1957), pp. 37 ff., and brought up to date in subsequent volumes.

1. Biography

BROME, VINCENT. *H. G. Wells: A Biography*. London (Longmans, Green) 1952.

DICKSON, LOVAT. *H.G. Wells: His Turbulent Life and Times*. New York (Atheneum) 1971.

MACKENZIE, NORMAN AND JEANNE. *The Time Traveller: The Life of H.G. Wells*. New York (Simon & Schuster) 1973.

RAY, GORDON N. *H.G. Wells and Rebecca West*. New Haven (Yale U.P.) 1974.

WEST, GEOFFREY. *H.G. Wells: A Sketch for a Portrait*. New York (Norton) 1930. Introduction by H.G. Wells.

2. Criticism

BELLAMY, WILLIAM. *The Novels of Wells, Bennett and Galsworthy, 1890-1910*. London (Routledge) 1971.

BERGONZI, BERNARD. *The Early H.G. Wells*. Toronto (Toronto U.P.) 1961.

——: *H.G. Wells: A Collection of Critical Essays*. Englewood Cliffs (Prentice-Hall) 1976. Includes the essays by Lodge, Pritchett, Weeks and West listed below.

CAUDWELL, CHRISTOPHER. "H.G. Wells: A Study in Utopianism", in *Studies in a Dying Culture*. London (John Lane) 1938, pp. 73 ff.

HILLEGAS, MARK R. *The Future as Nightmare: H.G. Wells and the Anti-Utopians*. New York (Oxford U.P.) 1967.

HYNES, SAMUEL. *The Edwardian Turn of Mind*. Princeton (Princeton U.P.) 1968, pp. 87 ff.

KAGARLITSKI, J. *The Life and Thought of H.G. Wells*, tr. M. Budberg. London (Sidgwick & Jackson) 1966.

LODGE, DAVID. *The Novelist at the Crossroads*. Ithaca (Cornell U.P.) 1971, pp. 205 ff.

——: "*Tono-Bungay* and the Condition of England" in *Language of Fiction*, London (Routledge) 1966, pp.214 ff.

MORTON, A.L. *The English Utopia.* London (Lawrence & Wishart) 1952, pp. 183 ff.

NEWELL, KENNETH B. *Structure in Four Novels by H.G. Wells.* The Hague (Morton) 1968, pp. 73 ff.

NICHOLSON, NORMAN. *H.G. Wells.* Denver (Alan Swallow) 1950.

ORWELL, GEORGE. "Wells, Hitler and the World State" in *Collected Essays, Journalism and Letters,* London (Secker & Warburg) and New York (Harcourt Brace Jovanovich) 1968, II, pp. 139 ff.

PARRINDER, PATRICK, ED. *H.G. Wells: The Critical Heritage,* London and Boston (Routledge) 1972. Collects reviews and articles on Wells published during his lifetime.

PRITCHETT, V.S. "The Scientific Romances" in *The Living Novel.* London (Chatto & Windus) 1946, pp.116 ff.

RAKNEM, INGVALD. *H.G. Wells and his Critics.* Oslo and London (Allen & Unwin) 1962.

RAY, GORDON N. "H.G. Wells Tries to be a Novelist", in *Edwardians and Late Victorians,* ed. Richard Ellmann. New York (Columbia U.P.1960, pp. 106 ff.

SCHORER, MARK. "Technique as Discovery", in *Forms of Modern Fiction,* ed. W. Van O'Connor. Minneapolis and London (Minnesota U.P.) 1948, pp.9 ff.

SHANKS, EDWARD. "The Work of Mr. H.G. Wells", in *First Essays in Literature,* London (Collins) 1923, pp.148 ff.

SUVIN, DARKO, AND PHILMUS, ROBERT M., EDS. *H.G. Wells and Modern Science Fiction,* Lewisburg (Bucknell U.P.) 1977.

VERNIER, J.P. *H.G. Wells et son Temps.* Paris (Didier) 1971.

WAGAR, W. WARREN. *H.G. Wells and the World State.* New Haven (Yale U.P.) 1961.

WEEKS, ROBERT P. "Disentanglement as a Theme in H.G. Wells's Fiction," in *Papers of the Michigan Academy of Science, Arts and Letters,* XXXIX (1954) pp.439 ff.

The Wellsian. The journal of the H.G. Wells Society (24 Wellin Lane, Edwalton, Nottingham, England.)

WEST, ANTHONY. "H.G. Wells" in *Encounter* vol VIII no. 41 (1957) pp. 52 ff.

WILLIAMSON, JACK *H.G. Wells: Critic of Progress.* Baltimore (Mirage Press) 1973.

823.912
Wel

39533

Parrinder,
H. G. Wells.

DATE DUE

GAYLORD			PRINTED IN U.S.A